New Psychedelia

Leif Podhajsky

D1546939

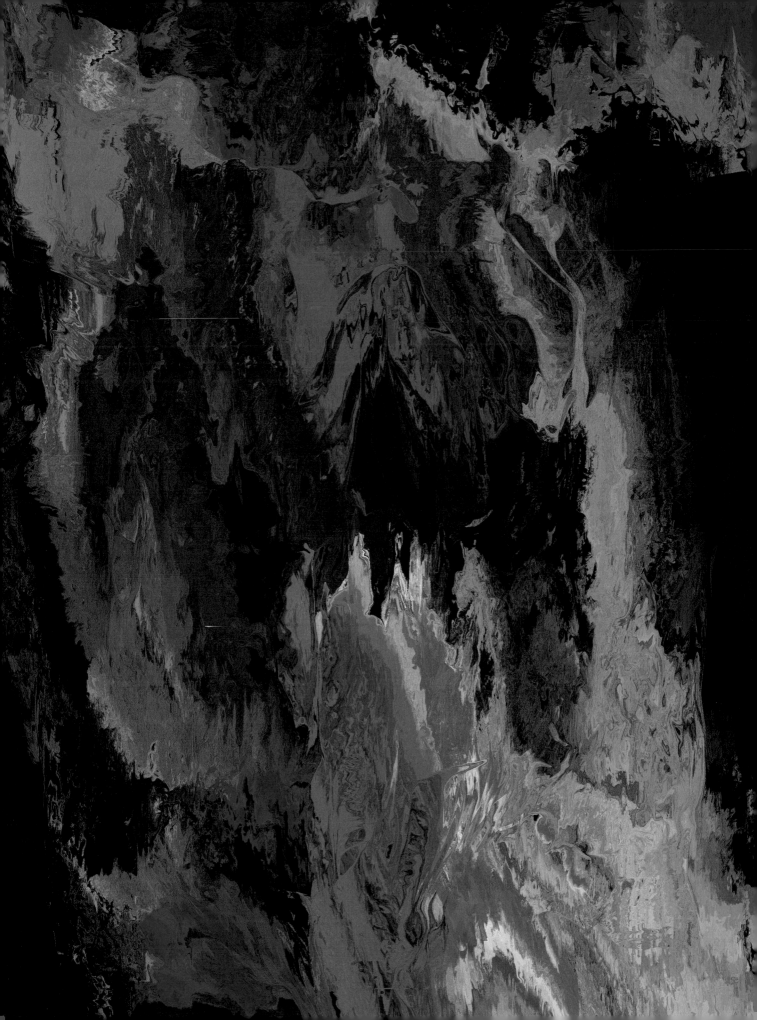

New Psychedelia

Leif Podhajsky

T&H

Texts by Evie Tarr

KEY

Vinyl CD Digital Poster Cassette

'To fathom Hell or soar angelic, Just take a pinch of psychedelic'[1]

F1

F2

Written by Dr Humphry Osmond in a letter to Aldous Huxley in 1956, this is the first known use of the word 'psychedelic'. The term, invented by Osmond, is from two Ancient Greek words – *psychē* (soul) and *dēloun* (to make visible, or to reveal) – meaning 'mind-manifesting'. Ever since Osmond coined the term, substances that have the ability to hold up a mirror to the mind's intricacies and potential – to show the mind to itself – have been categorized as 'psychedelic'.

In his book *The Doors of Perception* (1954), Aldous Huxley writes that '[t]he outer world is what we wake up to every morning of our lives, is the place where, willy-nilly, we must try to make our living. In the Inner world there is neither work nor monotony. We visit it only in dreams and musings...'.[2] The book is an account of the author's experience taking the psychoactive substance mescaline which, for him, opened a door to the 'Inner world' he describes.

Psychedelics come in many forms – from LSD (lysergic acid diethylamide, or simply 'acid'), to peyote, a type of cactus containing mescaline, to 'magic mushrooms', containing psilocybin, and DMT (N, N-dimethyltryptamine), which occurs naturally in plants, animals and humans. The effects of psychedelic drugs on those who take them are wide-ranging: from wriggling rainbow trails in the vision and the apparent movement of static objects, to nausea and dizziness or blissful, glowing feelings of contentment, to intense and cosmic – or hellish – hallucinatory experiences, with scintillating visual patterns and enhanced perception of colour. In the 1960s, these psychedelic experiences inspired a whole subculture in the visual arts and music – known collectively as 'psychedelia'. Leif Podhajsky's work represents a new wave of psychedelia that has its roots in the original movement but has grown to suit the digital context.

Podhajsky has created some of the most recognizable album covers of the past decade, for a host of well-loved contemporary artists, from Tame Impala and Bonobo to Lykke Li and Of Monsters and Men. Exhibitions of his fine artworks and creative collaborations with brands such as Nike and Ralph Lauren have helped to define a new era for psychedelia.

Humans had consumed mind-altering substances for thousands of years before the 1960s, but that decade has become synonymous in Western history with psychedelic counterculture. Funnily enough, it was also the decade in which psychedelics were made illegal in both the UK and the US. Today, a shift in popular opinion away from the demonization of psychedelic drug use is happening again, with new attitudes towards legalizing certain drugs for medicinal use, and a particular focus on mental health. Emily Witt notes the paradox in modern society's perception of psychedelic drugs: 'our culture holds two ideas of psychedelics at once, that they can be both serious and life-changing, or something you do on a Friday night to get goofy with your friends.'[3] CBD oil, extracted from the cannabis plant, has seen a huge rise in

Page 2
Devil Melt I, 2016

F1
Peyote, a cactus containing the psychoactive substance mescaline

F2
'Magic mushrooms' containing psilocybin, identifiable by their stalks, which turn blue when the mushrooms are picked

popularity, along with an increased interest in microdosing psychedelic drugs to treat depression and post-traumatic stress disorder (PTSD), and a push for education on safe recreational drug use with non-profit harm-reduction resources such as Erowid.[4]

LSD was first discovered in 1938, when Swiss scientist Albert Hofmann accidentally synthesized the drug; four years later, he discovered that it had hallucinogenic properties. Thereafter, it was central to 1960s psychedelic counterculture.

Musicians and bands such as Jimi Hendrix, The Velvet Underground, Nico, Pink Floyd, Janis Joplin, The Beatles, Jefferson Airplane's Grace Slick, The Zombies and many others began to carve out a new genre of psychedelic rock. A man named Joshua White created intricate liquid light displays, projecting light through moving oils of different colours on layered panes of glass, as a backdrop to the music of the time, known as the Joshua Light Show. Many other events contributed to the psychedelic counterculture, with its focus on the power of the individual as part of a universal whole – from Ken Kesey's Acid Tests, psychedelic parties in the San Francisco Bay Area, to the mass exodus of Americans to self-sustaining communes, a famous example being Timothy Leary's Millbrook. Of this time, Andy Martin writes that 'at the same time as biped Earthlings were being assimilated and integrated into some larger phenomenon, Gaia or the Force, they were also being split up, disintegrated, fragmented. Henceforth, it was ok to be an alienated, anomic outsider. But you could join up with any number of largely imaginary groups.'[5] The Summer of Love in 1967 is remembered as a crowning moment of the 1960s, with its slogans of freedom, love and peace, the latter involving anti-war demonstrations, and concern for the environment. Less well known is the long, hot summer of the same year with its months of protests against the many *threats* to freedom at that time – resulting in 159 race riots calling for social justice and protesting police violence across the United States. The Justice Department even asked local media to avoid covering the riots – an example of control over communication that isn't so easy to maintain in the digital age.

Today, the digital hyper-communication of social media platforms is feeding into movements voicing similar concerns to those in the 1960s. The fights for equality, freedom and the environment have been present in various forms throughout history, yet it seems these movements have been brought to the forefront again: from Greta Thunberg's *Skolstrejk för klimatet* (School strike for climate) and the rise of Extinction Rebellion (XR) to the increased visibility for the Black Lives Matter and Black Trans Lives Matter movements, to LGBTQ movements and anti-governmental protests. At the same time, it seems that the mindset forged in the 1960s, which valued the uniqueness of the individual while acknowledging that every individual is part of a wider whole – but then morphed into the profiteering individualist neoliberalism of the 1980s – is now returning in the form of mutual aid groups, self-organized grassroots movements and a sense of community heightened by freely accessible information.

Vibrant and hyper-real artworks – new psychedelia – are emerging from our interactions with the digital world and the dissociative effect it can have on us as human beings. Podhajsky's work embraces the possibilities of digital techniques, while maintaining a focus on the

F3
The cover of the January 1967 issue of the *San Francisco Oracle*, an underground newspaper reflecting and informing the psychedelic counterculture of the time

F4
A diagram of the effects of taking psychedelics by American psychologist and psychedelic drug advocate Timothy Leary. Leary coined the famous countercultural phrase 'Turn on, tune in, drop out'

F3

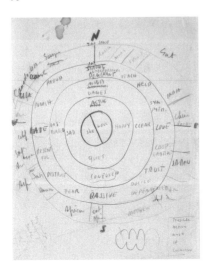

F4

human response. Like the liquid light shows of the 1960s, his artworks have been animated and projected on to the ceiling of the Sydney Opera House (see F6) as part of the Vivid LIVE festival, and have created the backdrop for live performances, such as the trippy mirrored image of cobras for Foals' 2013 set at Glastonbury Festival. The artworks themselves are immersive – often defying a particular focal point or definition of what the viewer is seeing.

Podhajsky takes inspiration from a huge range of artists. Japanese printmaker and graphic designer Kazumasa Nagai, whose poster designs use bold colours seemingly drawn from scientific diagrams, with shapes floating alongside the silhouettes of unfamiliar creatures, bright eyes peering at the viewer. The surrealist artwork of Russian painter and set and costume designer Pavel Tchelitchew, with his eerie 'Spiral Head' works where the human head and face are constructed from concentric circles that glow on dark backgrounds. The futuristic photomontages of Tsunehisa Kimura; and Andy Goldsworthy's intriguing and ephemeral artworks crafted from natural objects. The work of James McCarthy, Johfra Bosschart, Tadanori Yokoo, Kiyoshi Awazu, Vangel Naumovski, H. R. Giger, Michael Whelan, Carlos Cruz-Diez, Alex Grey, Takashi Koizumi, John Holmes, Mati Klarwein, Roger Dean, Wojciech Siudmak, Ljuba Popović, Pablo Amaringo, *Omni* magazine, Bas Jan Ader, Hieronymus Bosch, J. R. R. Tolkien, Rudolf Steiner, Caspar David Friedrich, Henri Rousseau, René Magritte and John Howe. Album artwork designers who have paved the way for Podhajsky's new psychedelia include Wandrey's Studio, Hipgnosis, Barney Bubbles, Stanley Donwood, Ron Raffaelli, The Visual Thing, Inc. and Kling Klang Studio, along with the futurescapes of Dan McPharlin, iconic Factory Records designer Peter Saville, and Storm Thorgerson, with his iconic *Dark Side of the Moon* album cover and his work for the likes of Audioslave, Muse and The Cranberries.

The world of Leif Podhajsky's new psychedelia draws on four areas of inspiration: synesthesia, nature, digital ritual and the Anthropocene. The first two aspects are already associated with psychedelia: synesthesia, altered perception of the senses either induced by the consumption of psychedelic drugs or, as in Podhajsky's experience, occurring naturally; and nature, which has always been closely associated with the psychedelic countercultural movement. However, the new digital rituals of day-to-day existence and the Anthropocene – the unprecedented levels of human impact on nature – have brought about a new genre of psychedelia that has evolved to keep pace with and reflect the fast-moving age of hyper-communication and digital dissociation we live in now.

F5

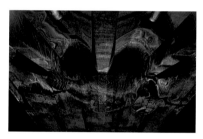

F6

1. National Center for Biotechnology Information, 'Humphry Osmond', https://www.ncbi.nlm.nih.gov/pmc/articles/PMC381240/ [accessed 20 July 2020]
2. Aldous Huxley, *The Doors of Perception*, Vintage (2004, first published 1954), page 27
3. Emily Witt, 'The Unpredictable Cactus', *London Review of Books*, vol. 42, no. 1, 2 January 2020, https://www.lrb.co.uk/the-paper/v42/n01/emily-witt/the-unpredictable-cactus [accessed 20 July 2020]
4. www.erowid.org [accessed 20 July 2020]
5. Andy Martin, 'In search of the Sixties: Was the decade really as good as we think it was?', *Independent*, 15 September 2017, https://www.independent.co.uk/news/long_reads/sixties-decade-was-it-good-sexual-revolution-swinging-london-hippies-culture-music-art-germaine-a7946506.html [accessed 20 July 2020]

F5
Leif Podhajsky at a climate rally in London, 2016

F6
Artwork by Leif Podhajsky projected on the ceiling of the Sydney Opera House as part of the Vivid LIVE festival, 2016

Opposite
Untitled 23, 2018

Overleaf
Dreamtime, 2016

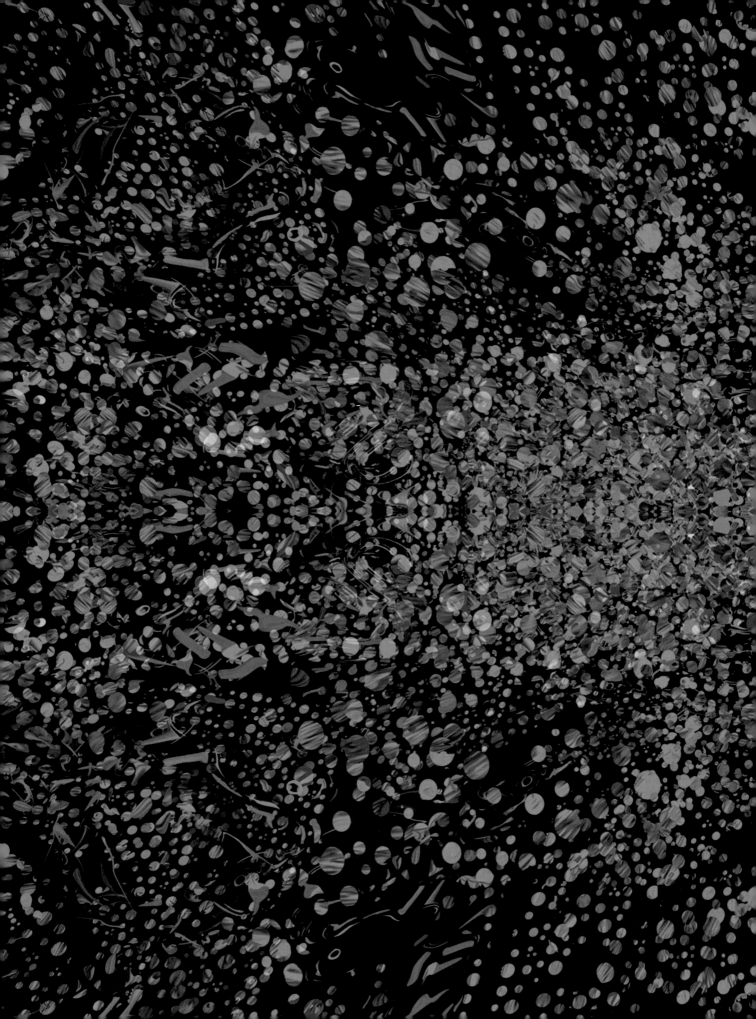

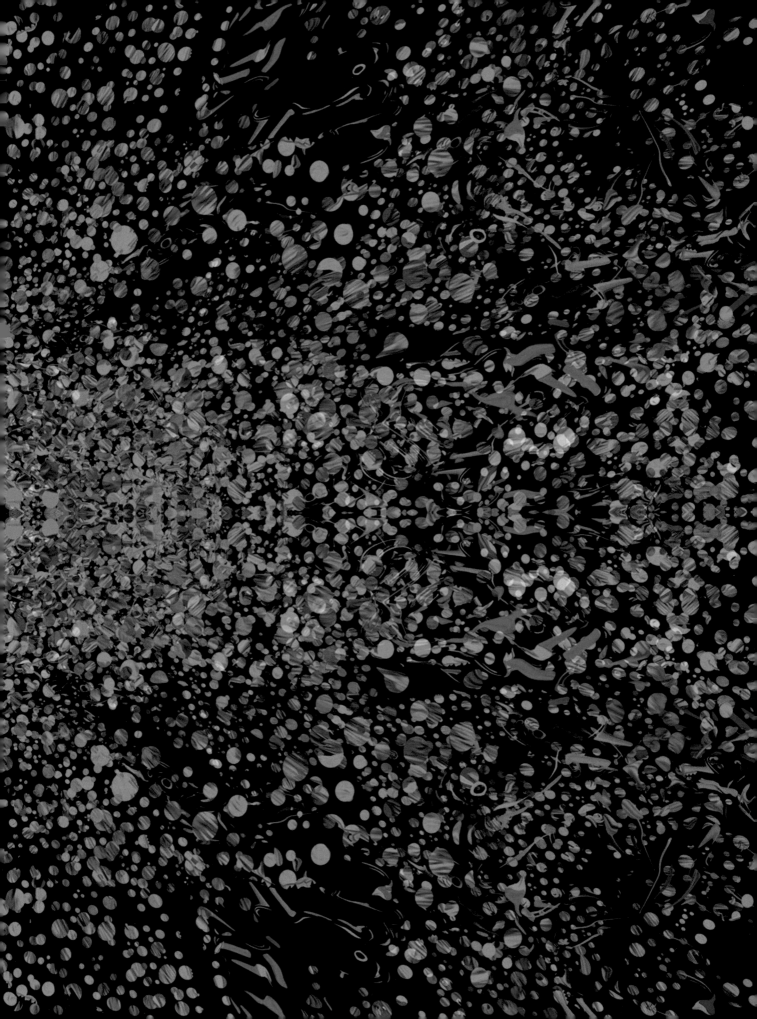

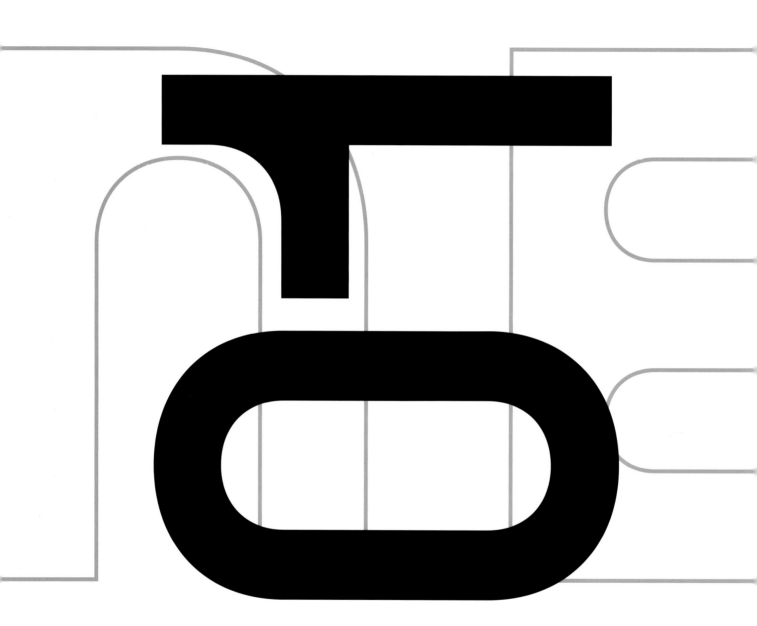

Tame Impala

INNERSPEAKER
LONERISM

[2010–2012]

MODULAR RECORDINGS

/ MODVL 128 / MODCD126
/ MODVL 161 / MODDLX001

As has kind of been the trend with my album covers, I just go with the first vision I have as a visual to represent the music. For this one it was this idea of an organically comprised photo of a landscape where some elements are stuck repeating into the horizon, like a glitch in the matrix or something, or when you stare into two mirrors facing each other. It's something normal and natural inside someone's mind bouncing around infinitely. I was obsessed with the representation of *inner* thoughts and sounds. I guess that's because that's how I saw my music as being different to the jam band music and communally made music that was happening a lot around me.

For me, [...] unless [the cover] was *it* it was useless. I remember starting to feel a bit down, like I wasn't going to get the kind of image I hoped for, until Leif came into the picture and started sending me works in progress, and I started thinking, Holy shit! It's possible! I'm seeing it! I obviously can't imagine the album without that cover now. I love the way it's 'natural elements messed with digitally', which is kind of how I appreciated the music then.

↪ **Kevin Parker, Tame Impala**

'I obviously can't imagine the album without that cover now. I love the way it's "natural elements messed with digitally"'

↪ **Kevin Parker, Tame Impala**

01

01

TITLE: *INNERSPEAKER*

YEAR: 2010

WORK TYPE: ALBUM ARTWORK

CLIENT: MODULAR RECORDINGS

MEDIUM: 12" GATEFOLD VINYL, CD, DIGITAL

TAME IMPALA

A

IT IS NOT MEANT TO BE
DESIRE BE DESIRE GO
ALTER EGO

B

LUCIDITY
WHY WON'T YOU MAKE UP YOUR MIND?
SOLITUDE IS BLISS

IT IS NOT MEANT TO BE

I wanted her
I wanted her
But she doesn't like the life that I lead
She doesn't like the life that I lead.
Doesn't like sand stuck on her feet,
or sitting around smoking weed.
I must seem more like a friend in need.

And I boast that it is meant to be, but in all
honesty,
I don't have a hope in hell, I'm happy just to
watch her move,
And in all honesty,
I don't have a hope in hell, I'm happy just to
watch her move.

And she doesn't like the friends that I make,
doesn't make friends for friendship's sake.
She just gets bored sitting by the lake,
her soul won't surface and her heart won't ache.

And I boast that it is meant to be, but in all
honesty,
I don't have a hope in hell, I'm happy just to
watch her move.

And I thought they could cure his disease, but in
all honesty, he didn't have a hope in hell, now
we'll never see him move.

DESIRE BE DESIRE GO

Feel it come
I don't know how long it's gonna stay with me
I'll let desire be
Desire go

Dare I face the real world

Everyday
Back and forth
What's it for?
What's it for?
Back and forth
Everyday

Everyday
Back and forth
What's it for
I don't know
I'll get out, won't have to...

Check my watch

I don't have the verve to belong to this dead side
Why I ever tried
I don't know

ALTER EGO

Said the voice from afar:
Don't you know it doesn't have to be so hard?
Waiting for everyone else around to agree, might
take too long.

When it won't be so hard, (it won't be so hard).

Well it's true,
yes, but you
won't get far
telling me
that you are
all you're meant to be,
when the one from my dream
is sitting right next to me
and I don't know what to do.

Oh alter ego.

Get them to love you,
while they may (Depending on your words and
wealth,
the only one who's really judging you is yourself).
Nobody else.

If I could part,
it wouldn't be so hard.

Well it's true,
yes, but you
won't get far
telling me
that you are
all you're meant to be,
when the one from my dream
is sitting right next to me
and I don't know what to do.

Oh alter ego.

LUCIDITY

I know where you went but I don't know how you
got there,
I know where you went but I don't know how you
got there,
Silver tongue hill where you talk up what I'd play
down,
I would speak up but I wouldn't know what to
say.

Lucidity, come back to me, put all five senses
back to where they're meant to be.
Oh it's hard to tell, it breaks down, there is a
will, there is a way.

Wondering around like spare time never knew it,
I might suckfizzle or I might just float away.

And we'll go running off tonight, high above,
where we won't even need to reach the sky, my
love,
Oh there will be a change in the air,
nobody will be anybody else.

Lucidity, come back to me, put all five senses
back to where they're meant to be.
Oh whose world do the overloaded fly,
down to the sea.

WHY WON'T YOU MAKE
UP YOUR MIND?

Am I
You'll

SOLITUDE IS BLISS

Cracks in the pavement underneath my shoe I
care less and less about, and less about you.
No one else around to look at me so I can look at
my shadow as much as I please.

All the kicks that I can't compare to, making
friends like you're all supposed to, but
You will never come close to how I feel,
You will never come close to how I feel.

Space around me where my soul can breathe,
Off-guard body that my mind can leave.
Nothing else matters I don't care what I miss,
Company's ok, solitude is bliss.

There's a party in my head, and no one is invit-
ed, and
You will never come close to how I feel,
You will never come close to how I feel.

Movement doesn't flow,
quite like it does when I'm alone.
I'll be the one that's free,
you and all your friends can watch me.
Today.

02

02
Gatefold artwork for the *Innerspeaker* LP

INNERSPEAKER

C

D

JEREMY'S STORM
EXPECTATION
THE BOLD ARROW OF TIME

RUNWAY, HOUSES, CITY, CLOUDS
I DON'T REALLY MIND

JEREMY'S STORM

(Instrumental)

EXPECTATION

Everything you ever told me could have been a
lie, we may never have been in love.
Stuck on thinking that there is always something
to lose, or a hit from above.

I don't need what I'm holding onto to.
I wish I knew.
But meanwhile

Fluctuations are aching my soul,
Expectation is taking its toll.
Fluctuations are aching my soul
'cause everything you ever told me could have
been a lie we may never have been in love.

And then I will escape, I'll never ever have to see
another disappointed face, no one to please. Every now and then, it feels like, in all of the universe, there is nobody for me.

I told myself I wouldn't care, no I wouldn't care.
But when she said she'd come round I combed
my hair, yes I checked my hair.

Fluctuations are aching my soul,
Expectation is taking its toll.

THE BOLD ARROW OF TIME

RUNWAY, HOUSES, CITY, CLOUDS

But don't remind me of home, there's every-
where I'd rather go.
It's true that some things have to change.

And don't remind me of home, or I might notice
where I am.
It's true that some things have to change.

I know some things have to change.

And gazing out the window, as I ascend into the
sky,
but I'm the one who's left behind.

There is nothing that is safe.
I know some things have to change.

Yeah, I do.

But don't remind me of home, incase it isn't
quite the same.

I DON'T REALLY MIND

Shifting, shifting, shifting, 'doesn't make so
much difference to me.
Huffing, puffing, marching around, like I know
how much better it should be.

I know it looks like I disregard the lengths of the
time.

But I don't really mind
But I don't really mind
But I don't really mind
But I don't really mind

Childhood puppetry for your hands
ants to give his
Pillar of strength death

TAMEIMPALA.COM / MODULARPEOPLE.COM

WRITTEN, RECORDED AND PRODUCED BY KEVIN PARKER, EXCEPT
ALL VOCALS AND INSTRUMENTS KEVIN PARKER EXCEPT DOM SIMPER
AND THE BOLD ARROW OF TIME, GUITAR ON INTERLUDE AFTER THE BOLD ARROW

ENGINEERED BY TIM HOLMES. MIXED BY DAVE FRIDMANN AT TARBOX ROAD STUDIOS
ARTWORK BY LEIF PODHAJSKY (LEIFPODHAJSKY.COM)

I had a pretty rebellious mindset at the time, which
helped me kind of shrug [the pressure] off. You know, like
'everyone wants me to do this so I'm going to make a
point of not caring if I give it to them or not'. A defence
mechanism, basically.

I sensed people's curiosity after the release, but not
connection. I was thrown into the world of music writers
and critics, so I probably paid more attention to that than
I should have, and not the people who were genuinely
loving the music. But I also didn't have social media or
anything so I didn't really have any connection with fans.

↳ **Kevin Parker, Tame Impala**

03

If [a new wave of psychedelia] was bubbling beneath the surface, I didn't know it! But I guess that's kind of the thing with waves that emerge – people are doing it themselves in seemingly isolated incidences because they're responding to the world they're in. Me and my friends believed strongly in what we were doing, which was largely anything psychedelic, but how that was influenced by anything else is really hard to say. We were so closed off from most of the world of pop culture. Modern pop culture, at least …

I was lost. It's so funny, because at the time I thought I knew exactly what I wanted, but looking back it's clear I was scrambling, desperate to discover elements (musical and non-musical) that I could call my own and forge an identity with. Getting signed to a record label gave me a bit of a boost and a sense of purpose, though, so I was able to stand behind ideas I had, for once in my life. The album art is a good example of that. I had an idea for a natural repeating wormhole thing and I was determined to see it realized.

↪ **Kevin Parker, Tame Impala**

04

05

03 | 04 | 05
Artwork for the *Innerspeaker* tour poster,
the 12″ vinyl and rolling papers

06

06

TITLE: 'SOLITUDE IS BLISS'

YEAR: 2010

WORK TYPE: SINGLE ARTWORK

CLIENT: MODULAR RECORDINGS

MEDIUM: 12" VINYL, DIGITAL

07

TITLE: 'LUCIDITY'

YEAR: 2010

WORK TYPE: SINGLE ARTWORK

CLIENT: MODULAR RECORDINGS

MEDIUM: DIGITAL, POSTER

TAME IMPALA   EXPECTATION

08

08

TITLE: 'EXPECTATION'

YEAR: 2010

WORK TYPE: SINGLE ARTWORK

CLIENT: MODULAR RECORDINGS

MEDIUM: DIGITAL

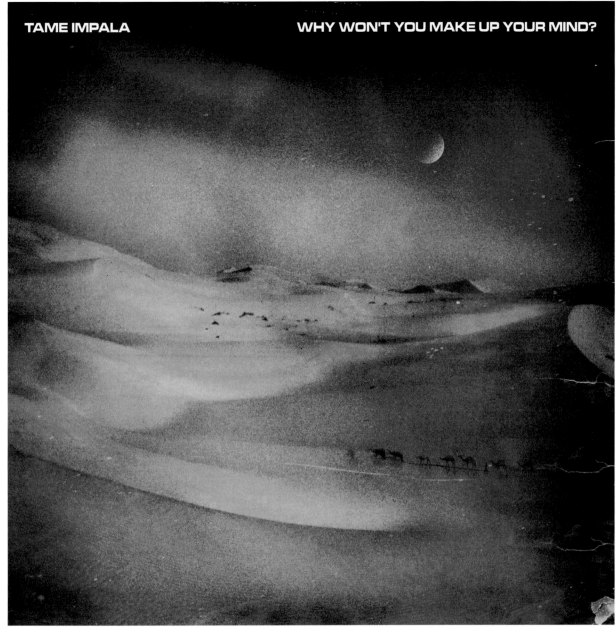

TAME IMPALA WHY WON'T YOU MAKE UP YOUR MIND?

09

09

TITLE: 'WHY WON'T YOU MAKE UP YOUR MIND?'

YEAR: 2010

WORK TYPE: SINGLE ARTWORK

CLIENT: MODULAR RECORDINGS

MEDIUM: DIGITAL

TAME IMPALA
LONERISM

10

10 | 11 | 12

TITLE: *LONERISM*

YEAR: 2012

WORK TYPE: ALBUM ARTWORK

CLIENT: MODULAR RECORDINGS

MEDIUM: 2 × 12" GATEFOLD VINYL, CD, DIGITAL

Paris has a lot of those gardens full of people lounging about in the sun with tall iron fences around the outside, particularly Place des Vosges, where I had the idea. I remember thinking it struck a chord with the word 'lonerism'. I also knew almost no one in Paris, so people being social looked *really* social. And the fence just seemed so brutal. This was actually my first idea, which I disregarded as I didn't think it'd work.

↳ Kevin Parker, Tame Impala

11

12

I was really into this idea of music for loners, or even just telling the story of the loner, which is something I had carried with me all my life and never really had a way of expressing – what it *really* feels like, etc. I originally thought this cover image idea was too obvious, like I was bludgeoning people over the head with it; the disconnect from normal, social people. That was until I saw the Jardin du Luxembourg when riding past one day. I snapped a quick pic with my plastic Lomo film camera, expecting to get a better one later – which I was never able to do. I don't know what it was about that day, but the park just seemed to be brimming with life, it almost looks like a film set. Looking at it now, I think the fact that people are all facing the sun, which is behind me as I take the photo, might have something to do with its engagingness.

↪ **Kevin Parker, Tame Impala**

13

13 | 14 | 15

TITLE: *LONERISM*

YEAR: 2012

WORK TYPE: BOX SET ARTWORK

CLIENT: MODULAR RECORDINGS

MEDIUM: 2 × 12″ GATEFOLD VINYL, 7″ VINYL, CD, POSTER

I felt *very* free. I actually changed recording methods to using a laptop, which allowed for many more sonic possibilities. I was very much exploiting that. I also had a bit of a kick of confidence to please myself in what I wanted to do musically.

↪ Kevin Parker, Tame Impala

14

15

TAME IMPALA
APOCALYPSE
DREAMS
—

16

16

TITLE: 'APOCALYPSE DREAMS'

YEAR: 2012

WORK TYPE: SINGLE ARTWORK

CLIENT: MODULAR RECORDINGS

MEDIUM: DIGITAL

17

TITLE: 'ELEPHANT'

YEAR: 2012

WORK TYPE: 12" SINGLE ARTWORK

CLIENT: MODULAR RECORDINGS

MEDIUM: 12" VINYL, DIGITAL

It was in December 2007, on one of my weekly Friday afternoon stops by Spank Records (RIP) on Bourke Street in Sydney, when I bought a kind of weird dance/edit record on a label I'd never heard of before from Western Australia. It didn't seem to me that anything was going on in WA at that time, so I looked up the label, Hole In The Sky Records, on Myspace and found out it was run by two guys – Ryan and Leo – who later became retro-flavoured dance project Canyons. I checked out who was in their top eight, and that was where I first came across Tame Impala.

I was listening to a lot of psychedelic rock at the time but nothing contemporary, so the tracks on the band's page really piqued my interest. I was messaging Kevin Parker on Myspace and eventually suggested they come 'over east' so we could meet face to face, and at the same time get an idea of what they were like as a live act. We booked the back room of the Excelsior, a pub just by the Modular office in Surry Hills, Australia, for a low-key mid-afternoon show.

↳ **Glen Goetze, Label Manager, Modular**

TAME IMPALA
ELEPHANT
—

17

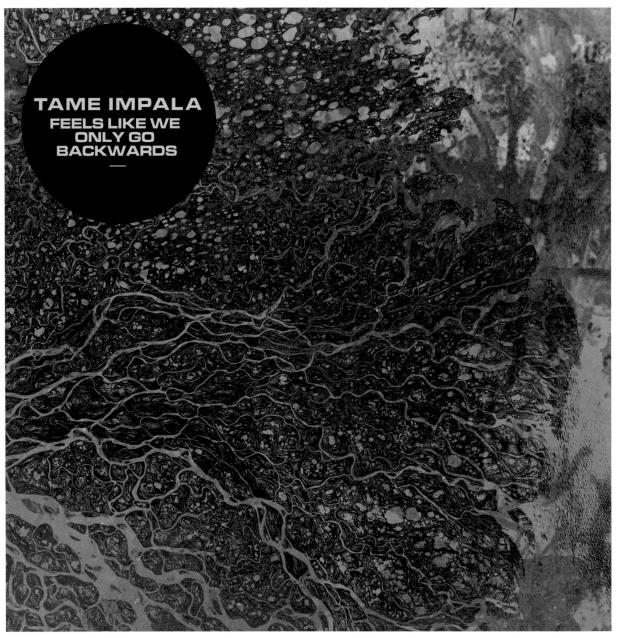

TAME IMPALA
FEELS LIKE WE
ONLY GO
BACKWARDS
—

18

18

TITLE: 'FEELS LIKE WE ONLY GO BACKWARDS'

YEAR: 2012

WORK TYPE: 12" SINGLE ARTWORK

CLIENT: MODULAR RECORDINGS

MEDIUM: DIGITAL

TAME IMPALA
MIND MISCHIEF
—

19

19

TITLE: 'MIND MISCHIEF'

YEAR: 2012

WORK TYPE: 12" SINGLE ARTWORK

CLIENT: MODULAR RECORDINGS

MEDIUM: 12" VINYL, DIGITAL

In the same way that Kevin was making psychedelic music in a more contemporary kind of way, I thought Leif's work did a similar thing with psychedelic graphics and imagery. It was psychedelic without being retro, which was an easy cliché we wanted to avoid.

↳ Glen Goetze, Label Manager, Modular

02

The Horrors

HIGHER

[2012]

XL RECORDS

/ XLBX 587

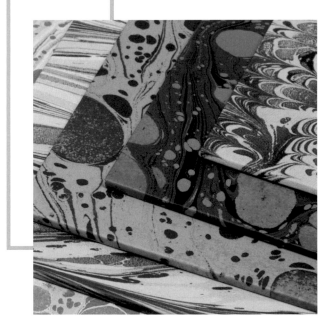

01

01

TITLE: *HIGHER*

YEAR: 2012

WORK TYPE: BOX SET ARTWORK

CLIENT: XL RECORDINGS

MEDIUM: 4 × 12″ VINYL, 2 × CD, DVD

The art direction for the *Higher* album artwork came from XL Recordings. I was asked to create some artworks to match the colour palette of the previous album, *Skying*. We wanted to create something that was toned back with block colours to give it a refined look.

I worked with Alison Fielding from Beggars Group and the band to come up with a set of marble artwork that would fit into the box set. The idea was to keep the packaging quite simple in tones and layout, with somewhat wilder artworks poking through in parts as you explore the physical packaging.

↪ **Leif Podhajsky**

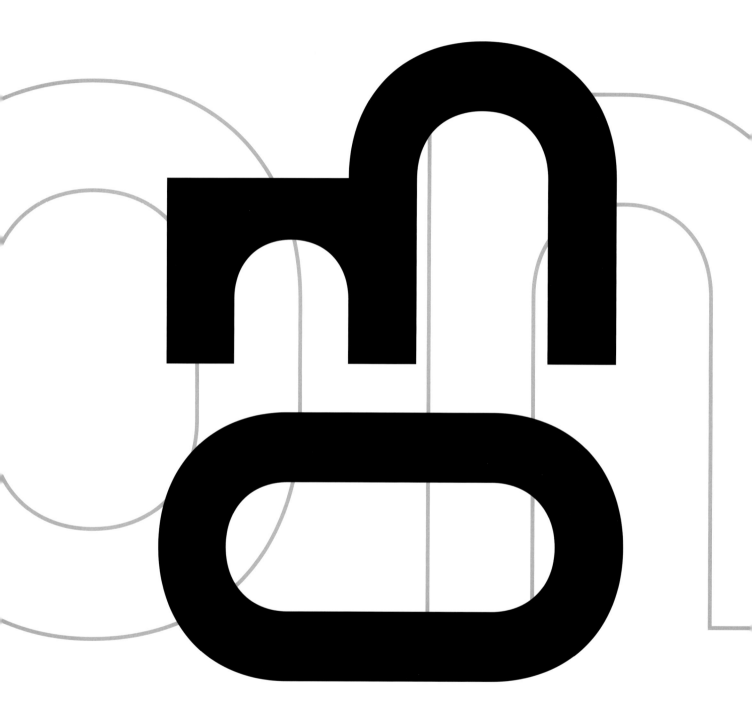

Bonobo

THE NORTH BORDERS
FLASHLIGHT
LES LÀ-BAS

[2012–2016]

NINJA TUNE

/ ZEN195 / ZENCD195
/ ZEN12409
/ ZEN12432

BONOBO

The turnaround time for the cover artwork for *The North Borders* was really short and everyone was a bit stressed. The brief was to continue in the same photographic vein as the previous album, using landscape photography to set the spatial mood. I put together a range of concepts which were mainly photographic but also, towards the end of the selection, I threw in a few surreal and dreamlike ideas. Which, ultimately, were the ones that resonated with Simon [Green] the most.

The image is an amalgamation of different photographic elements. I used some details of waves to create these shapes that envelop themselves. I then added different textures and adjusted the colours to create the illusion of mountains. The thing I like is that there's still a bluish hue to it that gives it a sense of mystery; somehow you can't quite place the setting. I think this really reflects the elements in the music: the duality of cold and warm, electronic and organic.

↪ **Leif Podhajsky**

'There is a warmth against cold that comes through in this album; the warmth I think comes from the feeling of live or humanistic elements juxtaposed with electronic ones'

↪ **Leif Podhajsky**

Bonobo
The North Borders.

01

01

TITLE: *THE NORTH BORDERS*

YEAR: 2013

WORK TYPE: ALBUM ARTWORK

CLIENT: NINJA TUNE

MEDIUM: 2 × 12″ VINYL, CD, DIGITAL

I love the whole of *The North Borders* record – the balance between the electronic and the organic meshing together in a seamless flow. I watched Bonobo perform it live at the Roundhouse and Brixton Academy, which gave me a sense of the detail and care that went into creating the album. There's a real sense of collaboration – different voices, different instruments and sounds all melting together to create this sonic dreamscape.

There is a warmth against cold that comes through in this album; the warmth I think comes from the feeling of live or humanistic elements juxtaposed with electronic ones.

↪ **Leif Podhajsky**

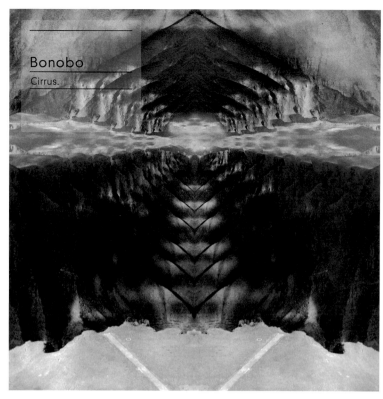

02

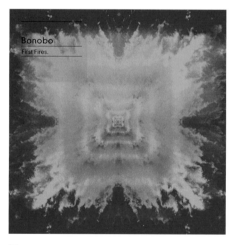

03

02

TITLE: 'CIRRUS'

YEAR: 2013

WORK TYPE: SINGLE ARTWORK

CLIENT: NINJA TUNE

MEDIUM: 12" VINYL, CD, DIGITAL

03

TITLE: 'FIRST FIRES'

YEAR: 2013

WORK TYPE: SINGLE ARTWORK

CLIENT: NINJA TUNE

MEDIUM: 12" VINYL, DIGITAL

Bonobo

Ten Tigers.

04

04

TITLE: 'TEN TIGERS'

YEAR: 2013

WORK TYPE: SINGLE ARTWORK

CLIENT: NINJA TUNE

MEDIUM: 12" VINYL, DIGITAL

I love to create a sense of exploration and wonder in my work. Creating worlds that touch on the balance between waking and dream, real and unreal. Creating a jumping-off point for people's imagination to take hold.

↪ **Leif Podhajsky**

05

05 | 06

TITLE: *THE NORTH BORDERS*

YEAR: 2013

WORK TYPE: BOX SET ARTWORK

CLIENT: NINJA TUNE

MEDIUM: 7 × 10" VINYL, CD, 3 × 20" POSTERS

Page 42
Artwork for one of three posters

Page 43
Sleeve artwork for six of seven vinyls

For the special edition I wanted to balance the photographic and surreal artwork with more toned-down graphical elements.

I created a set of symbols which I felt represented the album's balance and harmony. Something to add to the world that's created from the music and the cover artwork, lending weight to the universe it lives in.

↪ **Leif Podhajsky**

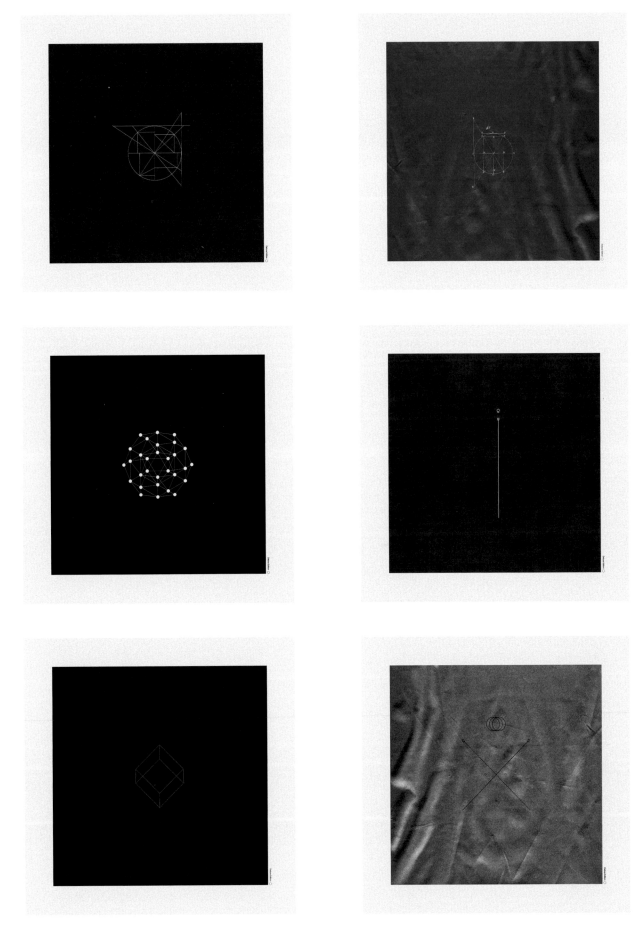

07

TITLE: *FLASHLIGHT*

YEAR: 2014

WORK TYPE: 12" EP ARTWORK

CLIENT: NINJA TUNE

MEDIUM: 12" VINYL, DIGITAL

My initial idea for the *Flashlight* EP was to create a transformative and bespoke object. We arrived at the idea of using a pattern comprised of tiny die-cut holes, using a new laser-cutting technique, which revealed an artwork underneath.

I wanted the inner sleeve to look like yellow and gold lava printed on high-gloss paper, shining through the holes cut through the matt-paper outer sleeve, like intricate lights emerging from the darkness.

↪ **Leif Podhajsky**

08

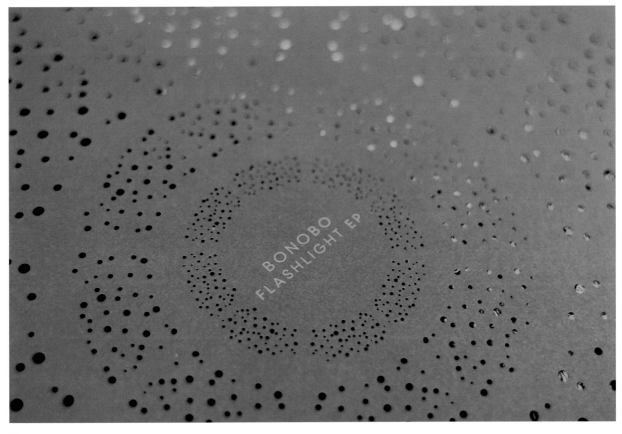

09

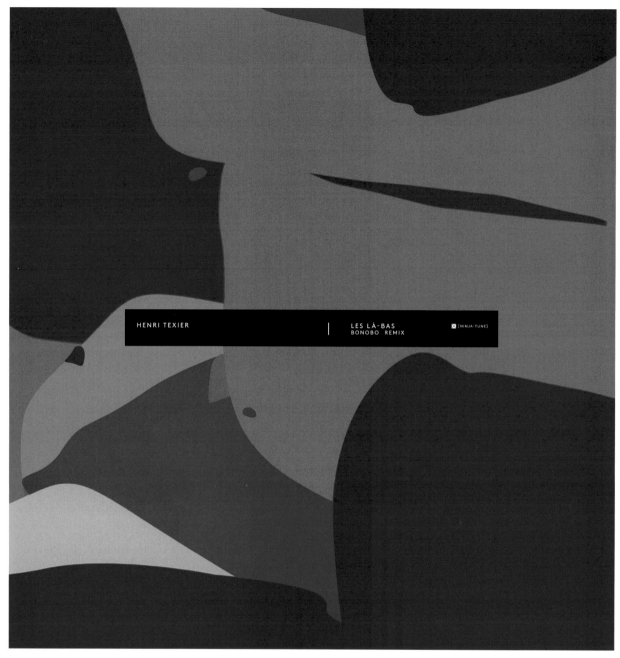

HENRI TEXIER | LES LÀ-BAS BONOBO REMIX   [NINJA-TUNE]

10

10 | 11 | 12

TITLE: *HENRI TEXIER - LES LÀ-BAS (BONOBO REMIX)*

YEAR: 2016

WORK TYPE: REMIX ARTWORK

CLIENT: NINJA TUNE

MEDIUM: 12″ VINYL, DIGITAL

Continuing on from *Flashlight*, with the Les Là-Bas Bonobo Remix I wanted to revisit the Braille idea and create an embossed pattern juxtaposed against a more abstract block-colour artwork. This gives a sense of reading the language of the music and the shifting elements that come from a remix of the original song.

↪ **Leif Podhajsky**

11

12

New Psychedelia

-8.5
5.0
FoV 188*250
210 *256os
Tra>Cor -14
>Sag -2

W 1078
C 589

DIA-S/RIL

synesthesia[HD]

SYNESTHESIA

TR=2.0 TE=30

Synesthesia

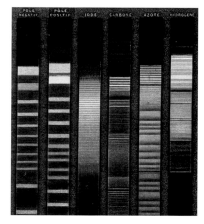

F1

Synesthesia is a neurological phenomenon where the senses of hearing, smell, sight, touch and taste can 'cross over' – meaning that the stimulation of one sense might have the effect of triggering another sensory experience. The word *synesthesia* literally means 'a union of the senses' – *syn* meaning union, and *aesthesia* meaning sensation. Although synesthesia occurs naturally in some people, it is also reported as a common side-effect of taking psychedelic drugs. There are many types of synesthesia, involving different combinations of the senses. These range from grapheme-colour synesthesia, in which people perceive numbers or the written letters of the alphabet each to be tinged with a specific colour, to mirror-touch synesthesia, where to witness someone else being touched makes the observer feel as though they are also being touched.

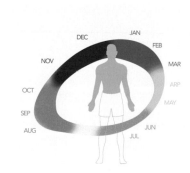

F2

Leif Podhajsky experiences two types of naturally occurring synesthesia: chromesthesia, in which sound causes colours to appear, and spatial-sequence synesthesia, where ordered sequences, such as months in the year, are experienced spatially. He perceives the months of the year in a circle that floats around a space in his mind. The months have different sizes and are roughly grouped in threes – with each group having a feeling associated with it (see F2). Reflected in his artwork is his experience with chromesthesia. When Podhajsky listens to music, the colours don't appear before his open eyes – they are much more hazy and intangible, like a dream: 'I have to focus on the feeling and colour in my mind's eye, like experiencing two worlds at once.' The colour is always there, but it is changeable and hard to grasp; indistinguishable shapes and warbling patterns appear and disappear. 'A light from the dark, something from nothing.' For Podhajsky, sounds are also closely linked to a certain feeling or mood. 'I've developed a strong relationship with how colours feel; I can sense if a colour feels right (to me). I completely trust this instinct and always go with the feeling rather than reasoning it out mentally.' It is hard to say when Podhajsky first noticed these crossovers in his senses, but once he began to create artwork specifically in response to music he began to understand his personal experience of synesthesia and, in turn, to channel his creativity through it.

Podhajsky's first experience of music came from his dad singing him to sleep as a baby. The chosen lullaby material would often be a whispery rendition of a song from Pink Floyd's psychedelic, fairytale-esque album *The Piper at the Gates of Dawn* (1967): 'Look at the sky, look at the river, isn't it good? Winding, finding places to go' ('The Gnome'). The lyrics accompanying the music are fantastical and descriptively visual, creating a pseudo-synesthetic effect of their own for the listener. Podhajsky describes the album as 'nursery-rhyme-esque but twisted through a psychedelic lens', and now sings the same songs to his daughter every night. The visual appearance of colour with music has had a strong influence on Podhajsky's style, and led him towards creating artwork specifically for music. For Podhajsky, music and visual art have

F1

A print showing the spectra of various light sources: solar, stellar, metallic, gaseous, electric by René Henri Digeon (1868)

F2

A diagram created by Podhajsky to illustrate his experience with spatial-sequence synesthesia

F3

A chart showing the nature of the synesthetic process

F4

A diagram by Emily Noyes Vanderpoel showing her colour analysis of an Egyptian mummy case (1902)

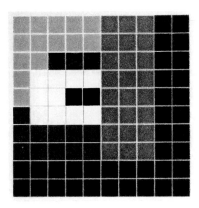

F3

F4

always been somehow tied together. The synesthesia-induced experience of music has flavoured his psychedelic style – linked to that indefinable crossover between the senses of hearing and vision. When approaching album artwork, Podhajsky listens to the music for which he is creating the work as a way to begin the creative journey. However, often the types of music that induce a more intense synesthetic experience are long, drawn-out and spatial-sounding tracks that tend to ebb and flow over time. In the past, people have tried to illustrate the correlation between sound and sight with experimental scales to show how colour and music harmonize.

'Both sound and colour are alike in that they elicit feelings and altered experiences in us that aren't wholly explainable or tangible. The difference in feeling you can experience from seeing a bright red in comparison to a deep blue, for example, or the way that music can transport you to a different time and place instantly, whether it be associated with a memory or some other dimension of thought. It can make you smile or cry. Sound seems to be rooted into our DNA, the soft thud of your mother's heartbeat or the hum of the stars.'

Leif Podhajsky

The creation of artwork for or in response to music is in itself a kind of symbolically synesthetic process – crossing the boundary between the aural and the visual. Both music and colour elicit inexplicable and varied emotional reactions from person to person – not unlike the psychedelic experience – and the intangible boundary, the meeting-point or the doorway between the two, has been a source of creative speculation and expression in many forms of art. The Russian abstract art pioneer Wassily Kandinsky famously made much of his work in response to music. Kandinsky's oil paintings, such as his *Musical-Overture Violet Wedge* (1919), often have darker lines appearing like staccato notes in a piece of music that cut through a flowing melody of colours softly clashing with one another and forming shapes. Kandinsky imagined the way people might *feel* colour as 'an echo or reverberation, such as occurs sometimes in musical instruments which, without being touched, sound in harmony with some other instrument struck at the moment'.[1]

The idea of synesthesia being a reverberation, with one sense touched by the ripple caused by the actual triggering of another sense, is a visualization that links closely to much of Podhajsky's artwork. Pieces appear to grow from a centre, or to be engaged in some kind of outward motion moving towards and beyond the edges of the frame of vision or the digital canvas. There is a sense of colour and shapes in motion, becoming alive and dancing to sound. In the 1930s, New Zealand experimental kinetic sculptor, filmmaker and synesthete Len Lye expressed the experience of chromesthesia in several ethereal and beautiful films, including *Colour Box* (1935), *Kaleidoscope* (1935) and

Rainbow Dance (1936), which show colourful shapes moving to music – large circles lit from behind expanding and disappearing, tiny polka dots flashing on and off, and hand-drawn squiggly lines shaking frantically. In a similar way, Podhajsky's abstract, colour-focused artworks seem to seize the motion of colour and sound in stillness – as though they were, in a moment, captured in the act of moving between the senses.

In 1671, Isaac Newton wrote that white light was actually a compound of seven primary colours: red, orange, yellow, green, blue, indigo and violet. Derek Jarman imagined Newton's moment of discovery in his book *Chroma* (1994): 'White light shattered into colour, Isaac in his closet, married to his prism and gravity with a little alchemy on the side.'[2] Some animals and insects have a heightened perception of certain colours to help with natural processes such as collecting pollen, reproduction, or avoiding poisonous plants and creatures. It is less clear as to why humans can perceive such a wide range of colours. Podhajsky believes that 'everyone has a unique perception of colour. Different cultures have hugely varied value systems for colour and I think this also happens on a more personal level … Each person has an affinity with certain colours, making them feel a certain way.' On the similarity between the experience of psychedelic drugs like DMT and that of synesthesia, he says they both can tap into 'a space that's outside our perceived reality. Psychedelics are a way to access this but meditation, dreams – when our brains can release small amounts of DMT naturally – exertion and breathing can all offer similar experiences.' Perhaps surprisingly, control and focus can be an important part of inducing an altered state of consciousness and breaking down barriers in the mind.

'I would say, for me, it's something that works best without a lot of other stimuli. It's easy to sense the colours and patterns when I am listening to music by myself. This is probably why I've always prefered listening to music alone rather than at gigs. I feel I always get a much more personal experience that way. I see why people go to shows to get that feeling, with the added lights and projections, to feel the mood of the room. I prefer to tap into it on my own.'

Leif Podhajsky

It is strange that a 'union of the senses', as is the case in synesthesia, has a divisive effect in a way because it emphasizes the uniqueness of each individual experience and the boundaries to full understanding derived from the subjective nature of perception. The way we try to narrow the gap between our various interpretations of the world, and make sense of colour on a universal level, is through the use of language. The nomenclature of colour has its history rooted in taxonomy and the study of the natural world, and is an example of nature helping to define or anchor our perception of the world around us. Early attempts to give names to colours were made by 18th-century naturalists such as Ignaz Schiffermüller or Abraham Werner, who devised a standardized colour

F5

A 3D view of the vessels in the eye of a healthy minipig. The hole at the top shows where the pupil, the gateway of all light, is located

F6

An illustration of 'Polychromatic Fringes' made using mezzotint with watercolour by René Henri Digeon (1868)

F7

An illustration of chromesthesia from Annie Besant and Charles Leadbeater's *Thought-Forms* (1901)

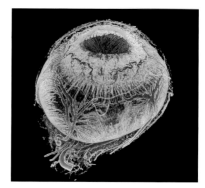

F5

F6

F7

'It's easy to sense the colours and patterns when I am listening to music by myself. This is probably why I've always prefered listening to music alone'

↪ Leif Podhajsky

classification chart, when they needed to describe the appearance of certain butterflies and other insects.

Podhajsky is always aware of the fact that the way he perceives his work is extremely different from how others might perceive it. Much of his work displays colour as though it has its own natural momentum, like water or cracked earth. Colour alone composes shapes and patterns – as if released from definition or categorization.

1. Wassily Kandinsky, translated by Michael T. H. Sadler, *Concerning the Spiritual in Art*, Project Gutenberg (2011), gutenberg.org/cache/epub/5321/pg5321-images.html [accessed 20 July 2020]
2. Derek Jarman, *Chroma: A Book of Colour*, The Overlook Press (1995), page 125

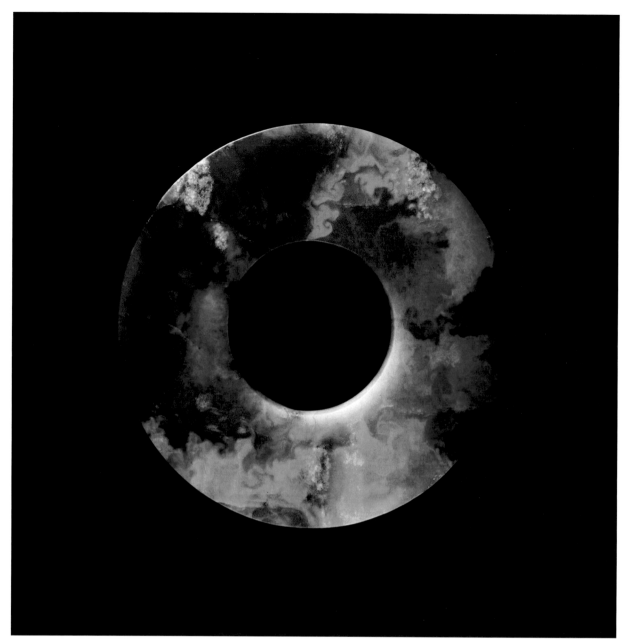

02

01 ↑
The Language Of Dreams II, 2016

02
Cyclic, 2016

03 →
Visual Impairment, 2018

'I have to focus on the feeling and colour in my mind's eye, like experiencing two worlds at once'

↳ Leif Podhajsky

Genetic Predisposition, 2018

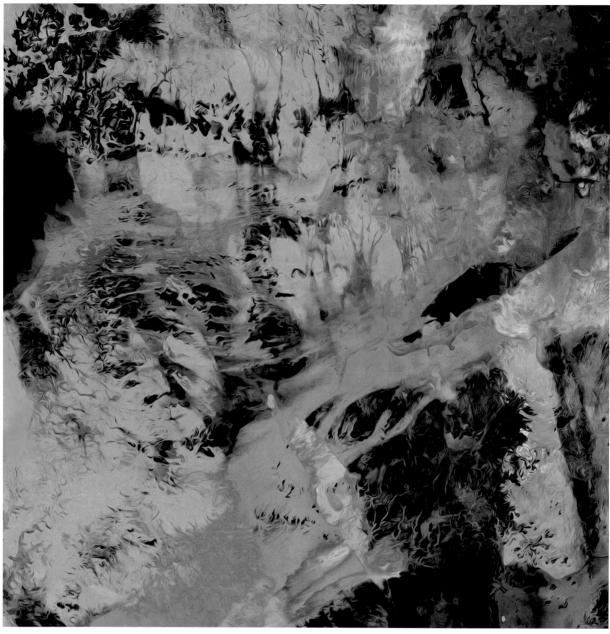

05

05

Synesthesia, 2014

06 →

Colour Shift, 2018

07 ↴

Night Cycle, 2016

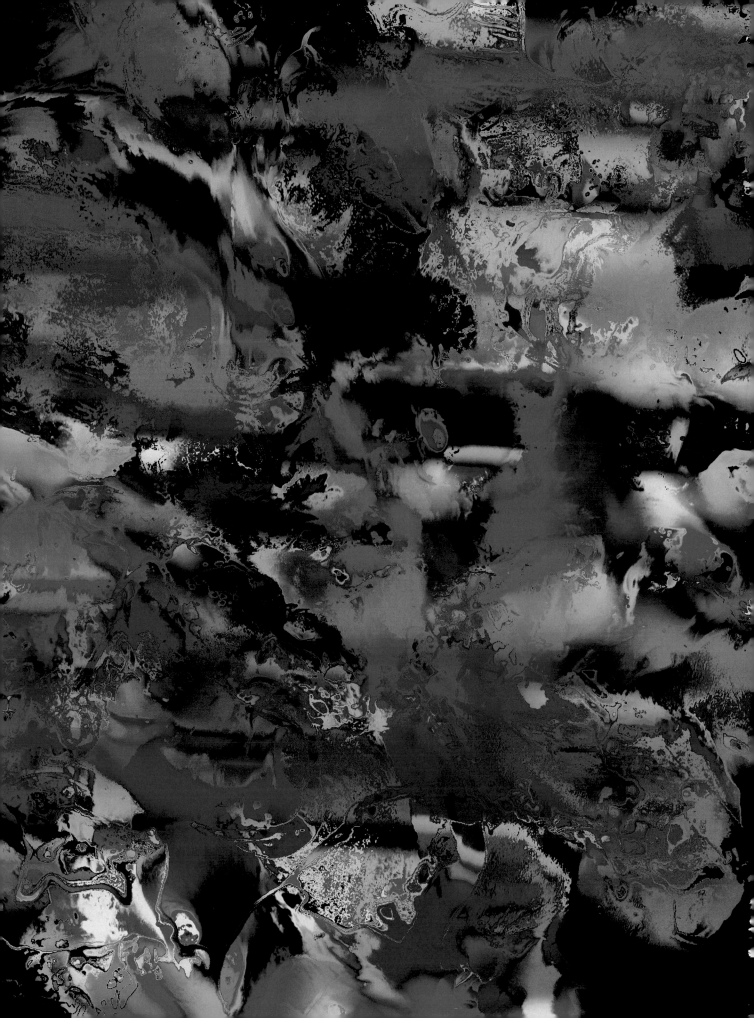

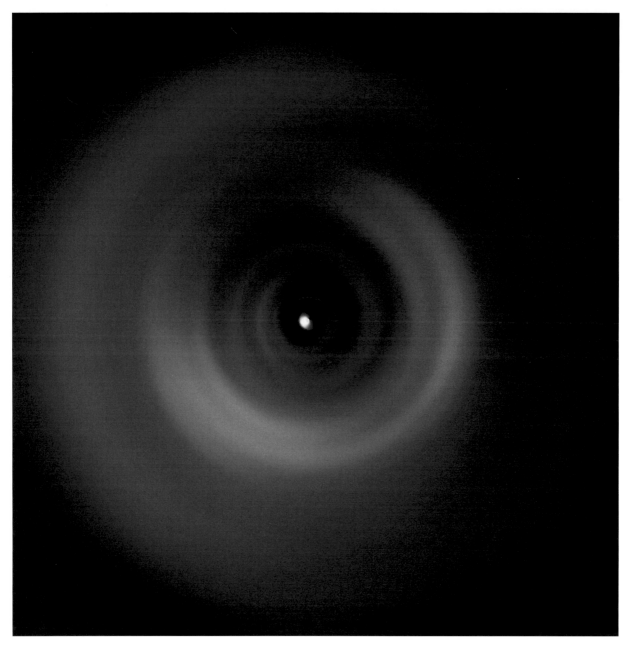

08

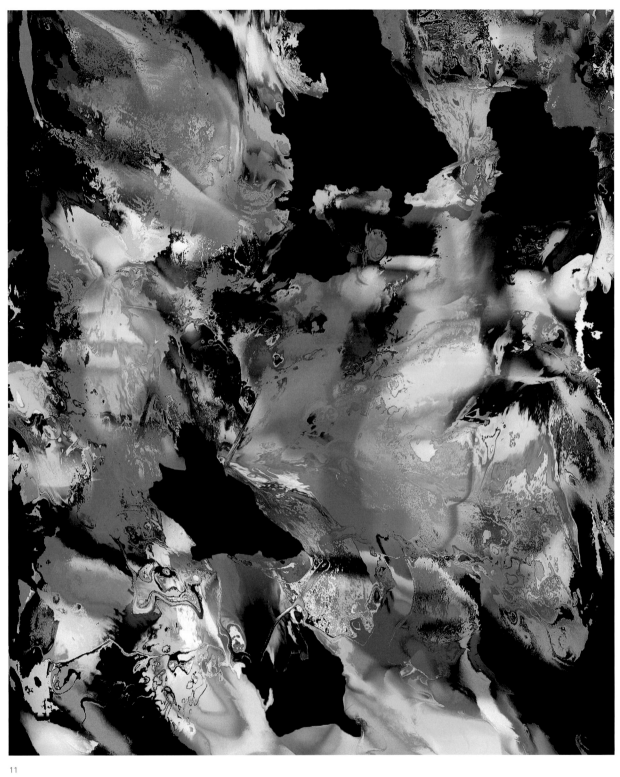

11

Primary Cause Of Permanent Planetary Change, 2018

11

Vivid, 2018

'Sound seems to be rooted into our DNA, the soft thud of your mother's heartbeat or the hum of the stars'

↪ **Leif Podhajsky**

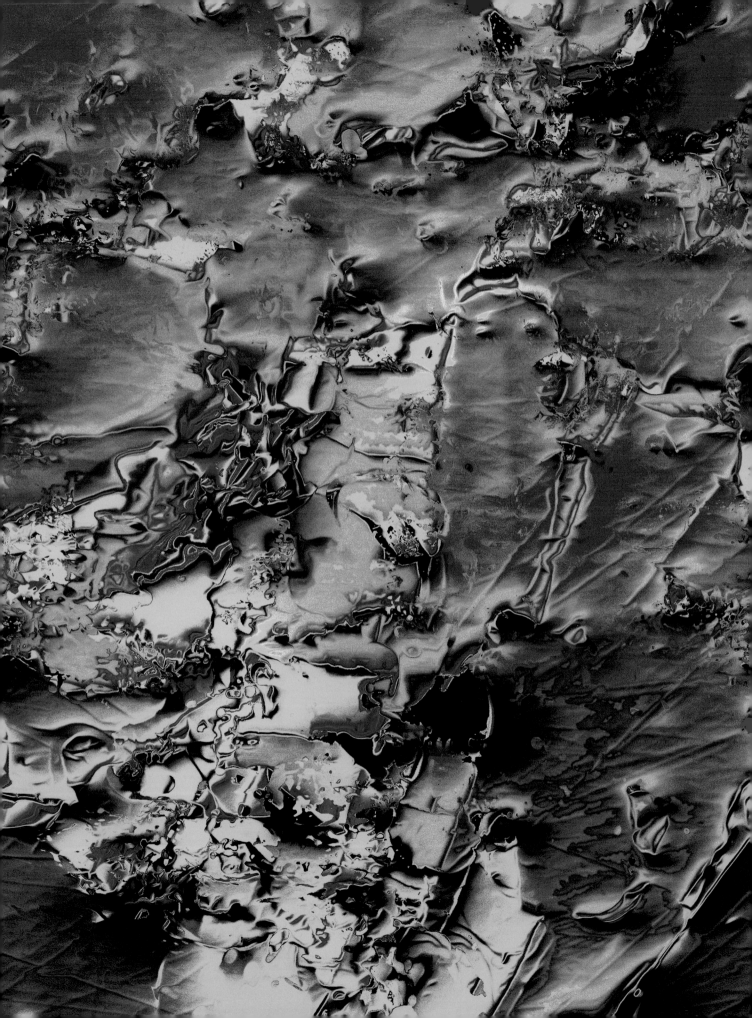

13

13
Dolby, 2017

14 →
Flow State, 2018

15 ↱
Fluffy, 2016

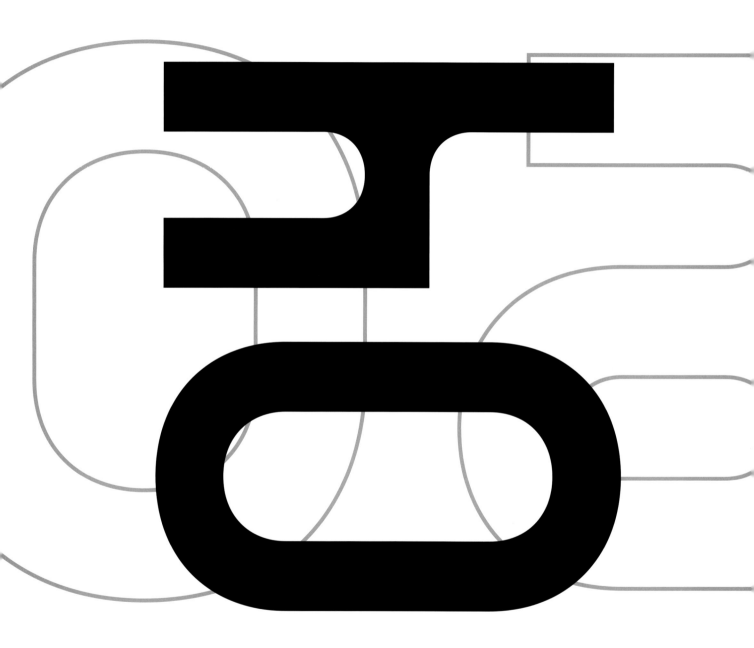

Foals

HOLY FIRE

[2013]

TRANSGRESSIVE RECORDS
WARNER RECORDS

/ LC14666 / LC14666
/ LC14666 / 825646521388

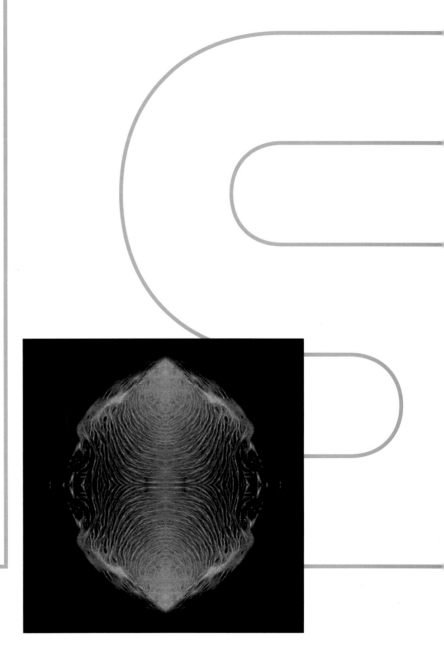

Early on in the process, Yannis [Philippakis] and I met at a café on the Kingsland Road, close to where we both lived at that time in East London. We discussed the artwork and images that he had been sending across.

Yannis seems to alternate between total piss-taker and super-serious in the same sentence, and leaves you trying to work out which one is which. I really liked that; I think as an Australian this really resonates. So there was some good banter and a rapport.

Yannis has always had a strong sense of how he wants everything to look. He would always send me loads of mood-board image refs. The final image we chose for *Holy Fire* is one that Yannis found and thought really suited the album. The brief for me was to try to give the image a new feeling, colour-wise, and also to manipulate it in some way.

↪ **Leif Podhajsky**

'The composition for me is what creates a sense of cinematic mystery. It's about what's outside the frame as much as what's in it'

↪ **Leif Podhajsky**

FOALS
HOLY FIRE

01

The original photo on the cover of *Holy Fire* was taken by Thomas Nebbia, a *National Geographic* photographer. We had to track him down to license the shot, and the shoot still remains a bit of a mystery as he didn't want to reveal too much about the image. I added the texture and colouring to match the old *National Geographic* faded feel.

The composition for me is what creates a sense of cinematic mystery. It's about what's outside the frame as much as what's in it.

↳ Leif Podhajsky

01

TITLE: *HOLY FIRE*

YEAR: 2013

WORK TYPE: ALBUM ARTWORK

CLIENT: WARNER RECORDS

MEDIUM: 12″ VINYL, CD, DIGITAL

02

02
Holy Fire CD label

03
Artwork for Foals' European Tour poster, 2013

FOALS
EUROPEAN TOUR 2013

[OCTOBER] 11 · OSLO ROCKEFELLER. 12 · STOCKHOLM BERNS. 14 · AARHUS TRAIN. 15 · COPENHAGEN VEGA.
17 · BERLIN HUXLEYS. 19 · WARSAW STODOLA. 22 · MUNICH THEATERFABRIK. 23 · ZURICH VOLKSHAUS
24 · MILAN ALCATRAZ. 26 · NIMES PALOMA. 27 · BARCELONA RAZZMATAZZ. 29 · LISBON COLISEUM.
[NOVEMBER] 1 · CLEREMONT FERRAND COOPERATIVE DE MAI. 2 · BORDEAUX ROCHER.
3 · TOULOUSE BIKINI. 5 · NANTES LA CARRIERE. 7 · NANCY L'AUTRE CANAL
8 · COLOGNE E-WERK. 10 · UTRECHT VREDENBURG. 11 · BRUSSELS CIRQUE ROYAL. 12 · PARIS ZENITH.

04

04

TITLE: 'INHALER'

YEAR: 2013

WORK TYPE: SINGLE ARTWORK

CLIENT: WARNER RECORDS, TRANSGRESSIVE RECORDS

MEDIUM: CD, DIGITAL

This was a photo of Yannis in a jacket he liked. I don't remember the context around it, just that Yannis thought it really captured the feeling of the song.

↪ Leif Podhajsky

05

TITLE: 'MY NUMBER'

YEAR: 2013

WORK TYPE: SINGLE ARTWORK

CLIENT: WARNER RECORDS, TRANSGRESSIVE RECORDS

MEDIUM: LIMITED EDITION 7" VINYL, CD, DIGITAL

06

06

This was initially created as an option for the back of the *Holy Fire* sleeve, and expanded on later to be used at live shows. The idea was to create a shrine – Yannis had sent some references for monuments with snake heads and I tracked down some images. I think this is from a Buddhist temple in Thailand, though I can't remember exactly. The snake was the central motif, surrounded by forest.

↪ **Leif Podhajsky**

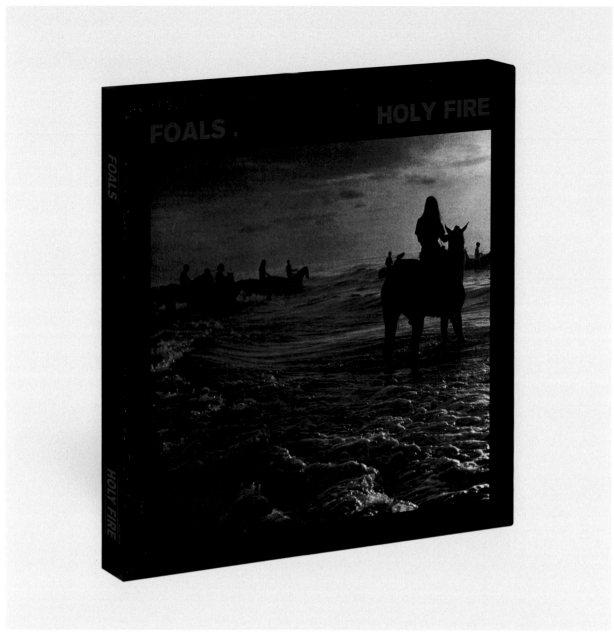

07

TITLE: *HOLY FIRE*

YEAR: 2013

WORK TYPE: BOX SET ARTWORK

CLIENT: WARNER RECORDS, TRANSGRESSIVE RECORDS

MEDIUM: 12" VINYL, 7" VINYL, CD, DVD

For the box set I altered the colours from the yellow/gold hues to a more green/blue gamut. We wanted this cover to perhaps feel more like sunset, while the original cover felt more like sunrise.

↪ **Leif Podhajsky**

08

09

Kelis

FOOD

[2014]

NINJA TUNE

/ ZEN205 / ZEN205CD

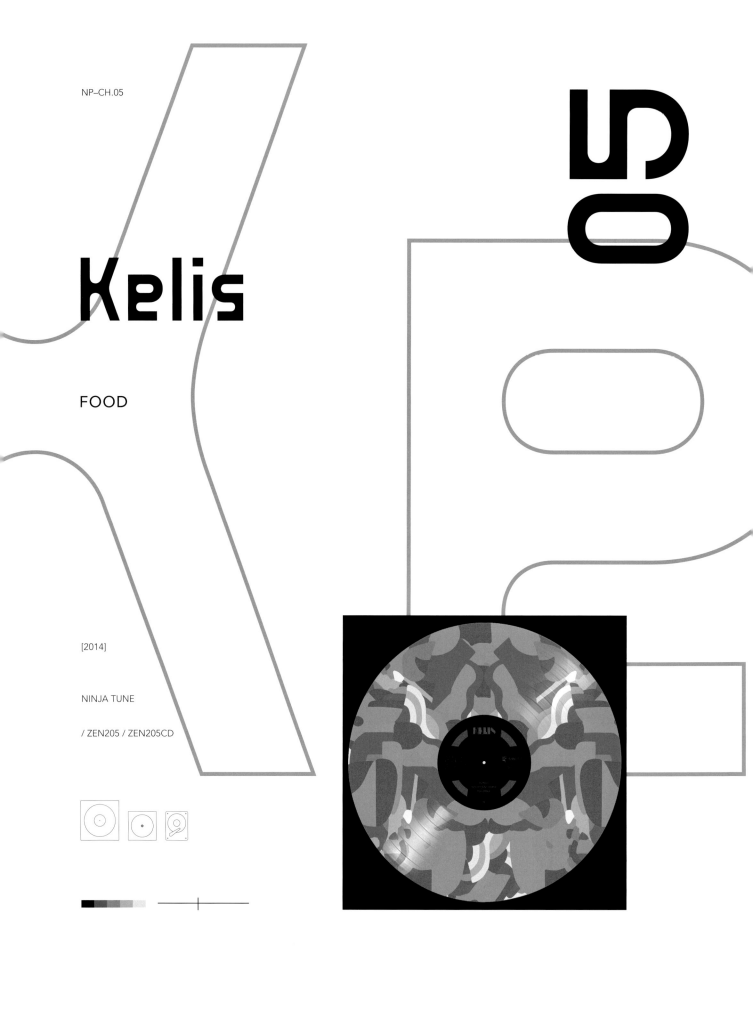

01

01

TITLE: *FOOD*

YEAR: 2014

WORK TYPE: ALBUM ARTWORK

CLIENT: NINJA TUNE

MEDIUM: 2 × 12″ GATEFOLD VINYL, CD, DIGITAL

Kelis really wanted to create a sixties vibe with this cover, which was a break from her other album covers. This album was a different approach for Kelis. She wanted to explore a more earthy, soulful sound, and working closely with her and Ninja Tune, I tried to translate this into a visual style.

↪ **Leif Podhajsky**

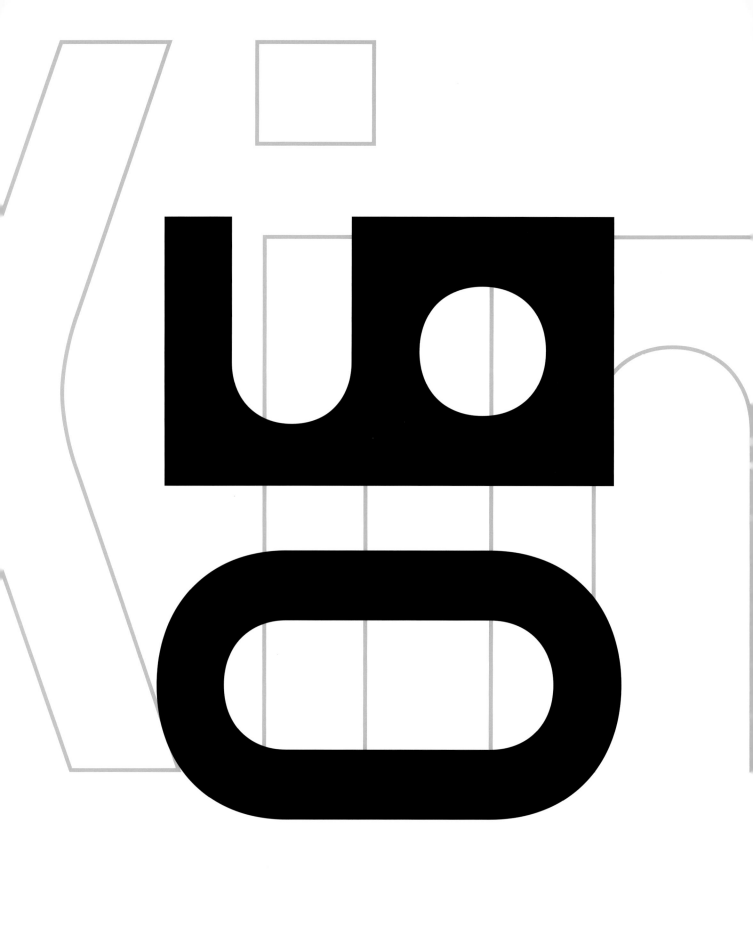

Mount Kimbie

COLD SPRING FAULT LESS YOUTH

[2013]

WARP RECORDS

/ WARPLP237 / WARP CD237

Before *Cold Spring Fault Less Youth*, everything we'd done had quite a cohesive visual identity that was more photographic, lo-fi and candid. We had a visual language, and I wanted this to feel like a break from that. The first thing I thought was that we should do something much more graphics-based that would allow a more abstract and open interpretation. And I remember wanting it to be quite distilled.

I had always loved the logos and sleeves of the jazz labels Blue Note and Impulse, and they made up a lot of the reference points I remember sending over. There were often figures or objects reduced to geometric shapes and presented in a way that was simple and bold but with a depth to them.

All that considered, I think what we ended up with was pretty close to perfect. In my mind, it's completely reflective of the record and intrinsically linked to the music and the time. What I loved about the final designs was that they felt like Leif's more psychedelic work, which we loved, condensed into a kind of anti-logo. It was organic (some people saw a heart, with arteries) but abstracted enough to create a new space for the album to sit in. It was a joy to then see that condensed version get completely exploded in the video for 'Made to Stray', which felt like a trip through the DNA of the whole thing. A brilliant exploration of the micro to the cover sleeve's macro.

I feel like people associate the record with the artwork that it came with, and it provided another layer to the record, one that expanded the experience of the album rather than narrowing it.

↪ Kai Campos, Mount Kimbie

'It was organic (some people saw a heart, with arteries) but abstracted enough to create a new space for the album to sit in'

↪ Kai Campos, Mount Kimbie

Mount Kimbie
Cold Spring Fault Less Youth

01

01

TITLE: *COLD SPRING FAULT LESS YOUTH*

YEAR: 2013

WORK TYPE: ALBUM ARTWORK

CLIENT: WARP RECORDS

MEDIUM: 2 × 12" GATEFOLD VINYL, CD, DIGITAL

02

02

Cold Spring Fault Less Youth gatefold artwork

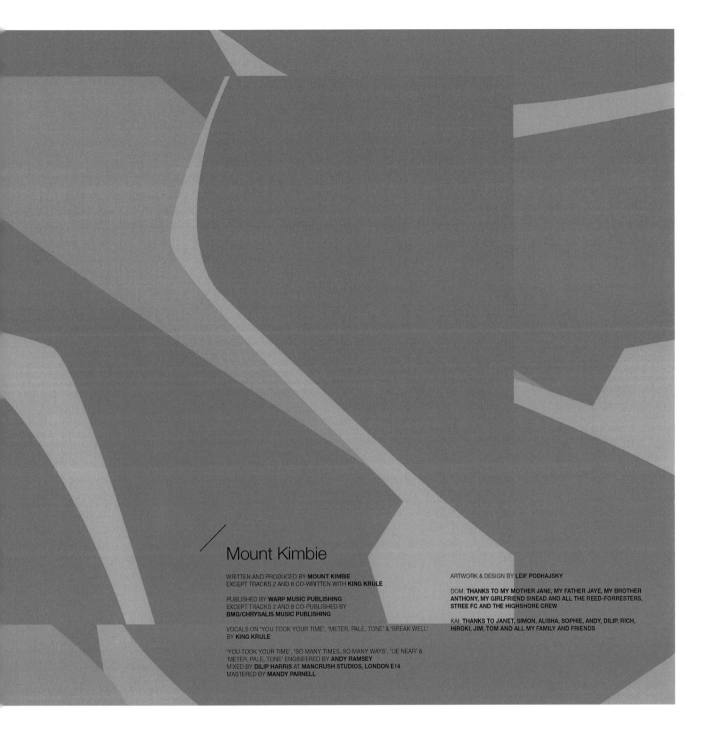

Mount Kimbie

WRITTEN AND PRODUCED BY **MOUNT KIMBIE**
EXCEPT TRACKS 2 AND 8 CO-WRITTEN WITH **KING KRULE**

PUBLISHED BY **WARP MUSIC PUBLISHING**
EXCEPT TRACKS 2 AND 8 CO-PUBLISHED BY
BMG/CHRYSALIS MUSIC PUBLISHING

VOCALS ON 'YOU TOOK YOUR TIME', 'METER, PALE, TONE' & 'BREAK WELL'
BY **KING KRULE**

'YOU TOOK YOUR TIME', 'SO MANY TIMES, SO MANY WAYS', 'LIE NEAR' &
'METER, PALE, TONE' ENGINEERED BY **ANDY RAMSEY**
MIXED BY **DILIP HARRIS AT MANCRUSH STUDIOS, LONDON E14**
MASTERED BY **MANDY PARNELL**

ARTWORK & DESIGN BY **LEIF PODHAJSKY**

DOM: **THANKS TO MY MOTHER JANE, MY FATHER JAYE, MY BROTHER
ANTHONY, MY GIRLFRIEND SINEAD AND ALL THE REED-FORRESTERS,
STREE FC AND THE HIGHSHORE CREW**

KAI: **THANKS TO JANET, SIMON, ALISHA, SOPHIE, ANDY, DILIP, RICH,
HIROKI, JIM, TOM AND ALL MY FAMILY AND FRIENDS**

At that time I remember feeling that working in conventional structures was a more interesting, radical change for us, and I wanted to see if we could do it. Looking back, I was taking the whole thing painfully seriously – which is, thankfully, very amusing now, but it was definitely a time that we were consciously trying to change how we worked. This record began a process of us playing fewer and fewer club shows and really moving in to a more indie, band kind of space.

The album process was definitely reflected in our personal lives as well; it was a bit of a time of upheaval. A good old-fashioned break-up and moving across the city (from south to northeast London, which may as well be a different city), away from what had been our lives for the last six, very formative years.

↪ **Kai Campos, Mount Kimbie**

All We Are

ALL WE ARE

[2015]

DOUBLE SIX

/ DS091LP

ALL WE ARE

01

01

TITLE: *ALL WE ARE*

YEAR: 2015

WORK TYPE: ALBUM ARTWORK

CLIENT: DOUBLE SIX

MEDIUM: 12" VINYL, CD, DIGITAL

I've always been fascinated with fusing digital and organic-feeling elements in my work. For this cover I painted a lone figure using block colours to add emotion.

I met with the band and we really connected; I felt I understood what they wanted straight away. We wanted to convey a vulnerability, but also a strength at the same time. I digitally painted this figure sitting on a chair and used different colours to convey the messages of the album. I love how simple and complex this is.

↪ **Leif Podhajsky**

Nature → N

Two young parents in a pale-blue Kombi van – with a fluorescent orange pop-top – are on a pilgrimage, driving to the coast of Queensland, Australia, to see the Great Barrier Reef. It's the 1980s and their two-year-old son Leif is in the back. In the years between then and now, the toddler has grown into the artist Leif Podhajsky, and the Barrier Reef has suffered considerably owing to climate change-induced mass bleaching. In 2019 it was reported that the number of new corals on the Great Barrier Reef had 'crashed by 89% since 2016 and 2017'.[1]

F1

Podhajsky lived in Tasmania until he was eight years old, then moved to the Northern Rivers in Byron Shire, New South Wales. Having spent his formative years surrounded by nature – and, over time, having witnessed considerable changes to the environment around him – Podhajsky cites the natural world and our impact on it as one of the key influences in his artwork. Byron Shire is an area completely shaped by the fierce power of nature – with the Indian Ocean pushing inwards from the east, and the 23-million-year-old partially eroded Tweed Volcano forming much of the landscape. Tweed was originally over 100 km (62 miles) in diameter and more than twice the present height of Mount Warning – which, today, stands at 1156 m (3,793 ft). Mount Warning is itself part of the remnants of the ancient Tweed Volcano – along with the green, undulating Lamington Plateau and the Border Ranges National Park with its hidden waterfalls and rainforest flora.

F2

Byron Shire has also been shaped for thousands of years in the human imagination. The Dreamtime stories of the Aboriginal people in the area have given deeper meaning to the land formations, infusing the dramatic landscape with thousands of years of imagination and belief. The Arakwai people of the Bundjalung tribe have inhabited the Cape Byron Headland – which they call Cavvanbah, meaning 'meeting place' – for an estimated 22,000 years, and are one among more than 500 Aboriginal tribes that inhabited Australia before the European occupation. In 2019, the Arakwai won a native title claim over the land in the area – two decades after they first applied. This grants legal recognition of the pre-existing rights of the 'traditional owners' of the land. It is non-exclusive, meaning others may still legally own and use the land, but it means that the people of the Bundjalung tribe have the assurance that they will be able to 'continue to be sustained by the ocean, to go out and fish, and beach worm, get pipis'.[2] The pipi is a type of edible clam, and is an example of how important the local wildlife is to the lives of the Arakwai people. The natural world is at the centre of Aboriginal values and beliefs, and this is reflected in the nomination of totems – animals or natural objects imbued with spiritual significance. The carpet snake is the Bundjalung clan totem, but the Arakwai also include *wajung*, the dolphin, *miwing*, the sea-eagle, the brush turkey, the pied oystercatcher and the turtle among their totems.

Being a subtropical region, Byron is home to a huge range of wildlife in its many habitats: rainforests, mountains, rivers, mangroves, tea-tree lakes and beaches. Podhajsky recalls plants such as pandanus, with its

F3

F4

palm-like leaves; grevillea, evergreen plants with bright-red spindly flowers like spiders' legs; banksia, wildflowers with orange and yellow cones that look like giant pieces of candy corn; flame bottletrees, tree ferns, kangaroo grass; and the classics: waratah, wattle and gum trees. Growing up, his favourite animals were green tree frogs, dolphins and kookaburras, with their distinctive laughing call and wings of mottled blue. His earliest memories were formed in nature – wandering through towering old-growth forests, and taking a trip to Cradle Mountain in Tasmania with his family. An old converted bus with an extra room built on the side was his first home, with an outdoor bathtub heated by a wood fire and overlooking the forest. The family later moved into a house surrounded by a giant wild hedge, a block away from the ocean.

'The sea is always with me, it was such a big part of my life for so long. At one point I felt so comfortable and in tune with its cycles that it felt as familiar for me to be in it as it was to be on land. It was the centre of all our activity as kids, but I've always been respectful and somewhat cautious around it; especially in Australia it can be super-dangerous, so trying to learn and get comfortable was my way of understanding and not being so afraid.'

Leif Podhajsky

On the Byron Shire coast, jagged land tapers off at the edges where the harsh punctuation of rock meets the flat calmness of the sea. Cape Byron Light, a stately white lighthouse built between 1899 and 1901, perches on the headland. Its lantern is the most powerful in Australia, and serves as a reminder that the sea is a force of natural chaos that defies human logic – we can watch and warn, but there's no hope of controlling it. Aged 15, drawn to the paradoxical furious energy and calm beauty of the sea, Podhajsky chose to study marine biology at school. Open-sea dive training was part of the course. Being under the sea is in itself like entering a different plane of existence, where dry-land communication methods are rendered either impossible or greatly changed. It is a humbling and peculiar feeling to be sitting on the sea bed with a crystal clear block on top of you. With 30 m (98 ft) up to the surface, when you're down that deep it's dark – you can only *just* see your hands stretched out in front of you. Communication disintegrates; all that can be heard is your own breath and the rushing, burbling, clicking noises of the ocean. The sea summates the great power of a natural force in contrast to any single individual, and to dive in open water is to be a guest in an environment that has grown unfamiliar to us since we crawled from it in our earliest forms around 530 million years ago.

'Everything in nature invites us constantly to be what we are.'

Gretel Ehrlich[3]

The two-sided discourse around global warming and the environment can make us forget that we are not separate from nature, we *are* ourselves a part of it. Much is written and spoken about human impact – 'us', on the planet, 'it' – but there is simply no distinction between 'us' and 'it'. We are nature, and by harming the planet we are also harming ourselves. Among the most frequently reproduced photographs in history is one of the earliest colour photographs taken of planet Earth – the picture is called 'The Blue Marble', and it was taken by the Apollo crew in 1972. As humans, our ability to view the natural world from an outside perspective, combined with our obsessive self-awareness, can place us at a remove from nature. For those who have grown up surrounded by nature, though, it's hard to shake the yearning to return to it. Podhajsky constantly reminds himself of nature's importance, and his artwork reflects this. His mantra is that we are all one and the same thing, and to reconnect with nature is to bring about a real sense of harmony. His work is full of patterns derived from nature; of recreating and drawing inspiration from these intricate forms he says, 'the patterns we mimic are just as much in us as in the other parts of nature'.

Plants aren't so different from people. Like us, many types of plant measure time using an inbuilt circadian clock, tuned in to the 24-hour rotation of the Earth on its axis, taking cues from the sun to determine the day or the time of year. Some flowers, such as evening primrose and moonflower, bloom only in the evening, curling back their petals for moths and other nocturnal pollinators.

And there are many quiet, busy and integral forms of intelligence in nature that pass under our radar. Take mycelium (see F6) – the part of a fungus that collects nutrients from its surroundings. It has many tiny branches or filaments containing bundles of nuclei that feed information found at the tips of each branch – maybe the discovery of a particularly tasty mineral rock – to the rest of the branches, a bit like sensors on the body reporting back to the brain. Mycelium is essential to the ecosystem, as it helps to decompose plant material. Interestingly, like us, mycelium absorbs oxygen and releases carbon dioxide. According to mycologist Paul Stamets, though, human beings tend to see fungi as particularly alien and mysterious. His reasoning for this is that mushrooms are something that can 'kill you, that can feed you, that can take you on a spiritual journey and grow then be gone within five days'.[4]

When something can defy the comfort of human structures and boundaries, and can also break down those limits within the mind, it can feel alien to us – but perhaps a closer relationship with nature will bring us back to the selves that exist apart from societal structures. In the past, studies have looked to connect an understanding of ecology with psychedelics. Ralph Metzner, an American psychologist, even argued that psychedelic drug use was the impetus for the environmental movements of the 1960s. Although this seems far-fetched, it does appear that there is a connection between the disorder and chaos of nature and the ability of psychedelics to break down human-imposed structures of thought to enable a keener understanding of the self as part of a natural whole.

F5
Australian wildflowers

F6
Mycelium in a petri dish

F7
Illustrative plate from Nehemiah Grew's *The Anatomy of Plants* (1682)

F5

F6

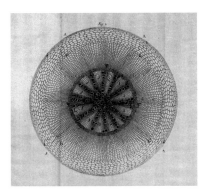

F7

Podhajsky's work seeks to express and elevate the chaotic beauty of nature through a lens of psychedelia – either defying conventional structure and the comfort of repetition, or leaning into it by imposing artifical order on the disorder of natural form. The jagged reflection of a mountain range hits the surface of a glassy lake and melts into globular curves, while antiquated petals and leaves of flowers are cloned and arranged to crowd around an empty centre. Here, unnaturally vivid colours seem almost to pulsate among forms that may or may not be feathers, moving water or part of an organism under a microscope. Today, fast-paced inner-city life is widening the perceived gap between us and the natural world. Now living in Berlin, Podhajsky often feels the need to return to nature – making journeys to go climbing or free camping; to Snowdonia and to the Lake District. His work, combining natural subjects with digital processes, reflects how our own natural rhythms are being changed by digital life. The circadian clock is interrupted by artificial light as we work and communicate into the night – while our ways of socializing with others and perceiving ourselves have changed greatly. It can be disorienting and uncanny – like the unidentifiable forms in Podhajsky's work – causing us to turn back towards the natural forms we know for guidance and understanding.

1. Lisa Cox, 'Great Barrier Reef suffers 89% collapse in new coral after bleaching events', *Guardian*, 3 April 2019, https://www.theguardian.com/environment/2019/apr/04/great-barrier-reef-suffers-89-collapse-in-new-coral-after-bleaching-events [accessed 21 July 2020]
2. Hannah Ross, Elloise Farrow-Smith and Bronwyn Herbert, 'Byron Bay's Bundjalung people celebrate long-awaited land and sea native title determination', ABC News, 30 April 2019, https://www.abc.net.au/news/2019-04-30/byron-bay-native-title-land-rights/11057896 [accessed 21 July 2020]
3. Gretel Ehrlich, *The Solace of Open Spaces*, Penguin (1986), page 108
4. Paul Stamets, 'Mushrooms, Mycology of Consciousness', EcoFarm Conference Keynote, 2017, https://www.youtube.com/watch?v=t8DjeaU8eMs [accessed 21 July 2020]

'There are many quiet, busy and integral forms of intelligence in nature that pass under our radar'

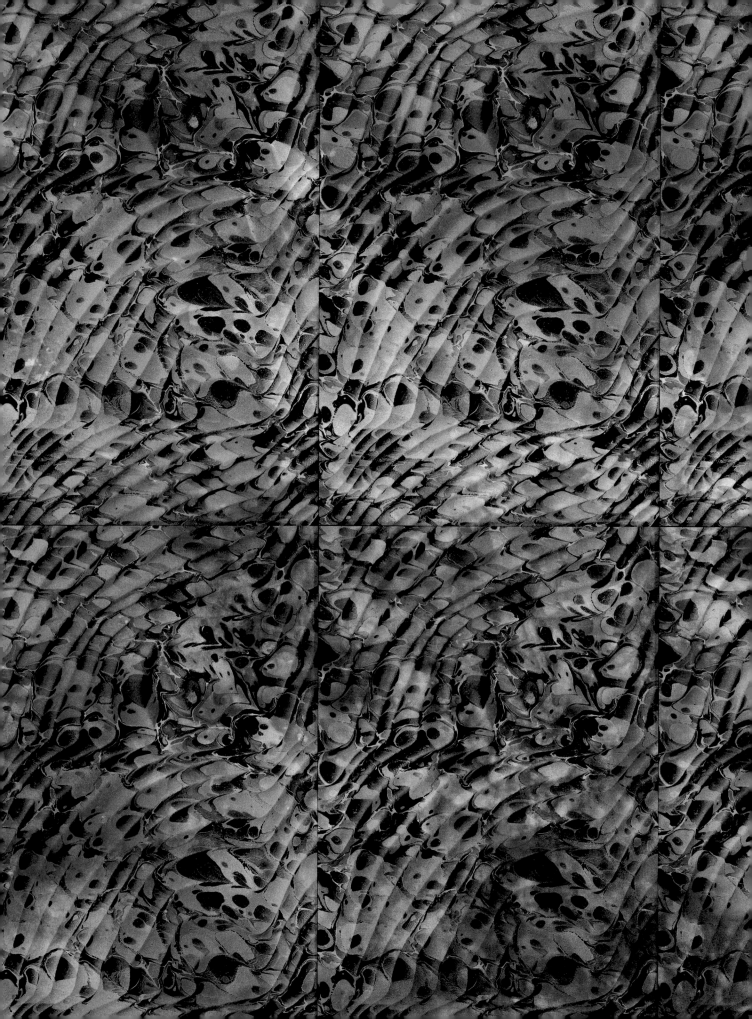

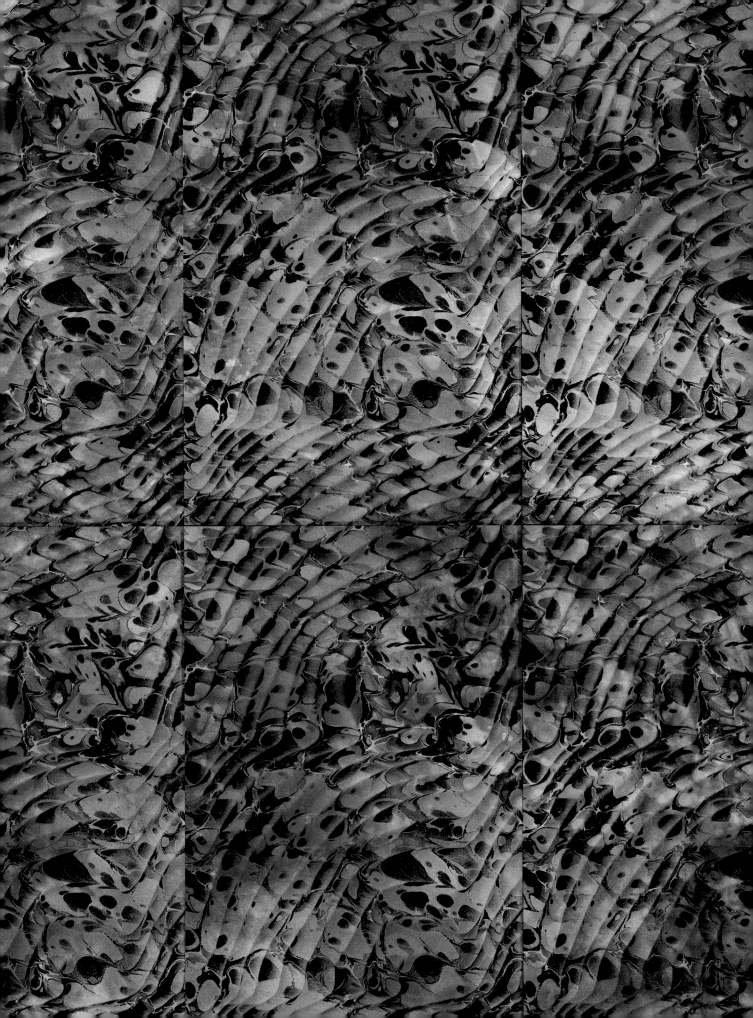

02

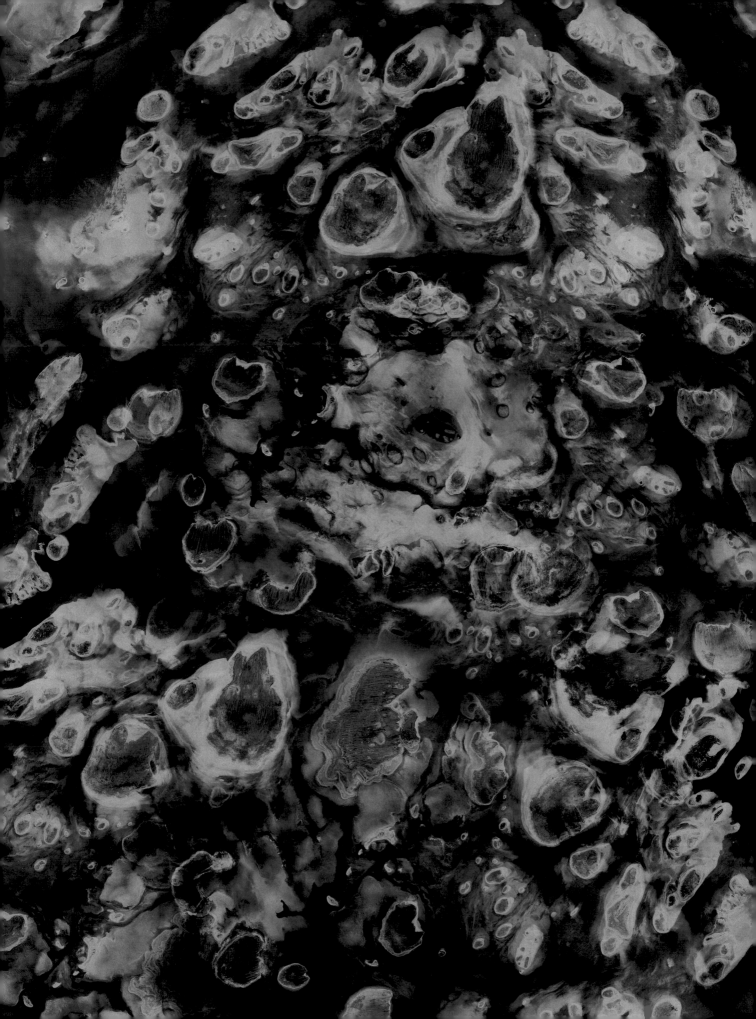

'The sea is always with me, it was such a big part of my life for so long. At one point I felt so comfortable and in tune with its cycles that it felt as familiar for me to be in it as it was to be on land'

↪ **Leif Podhajsky**

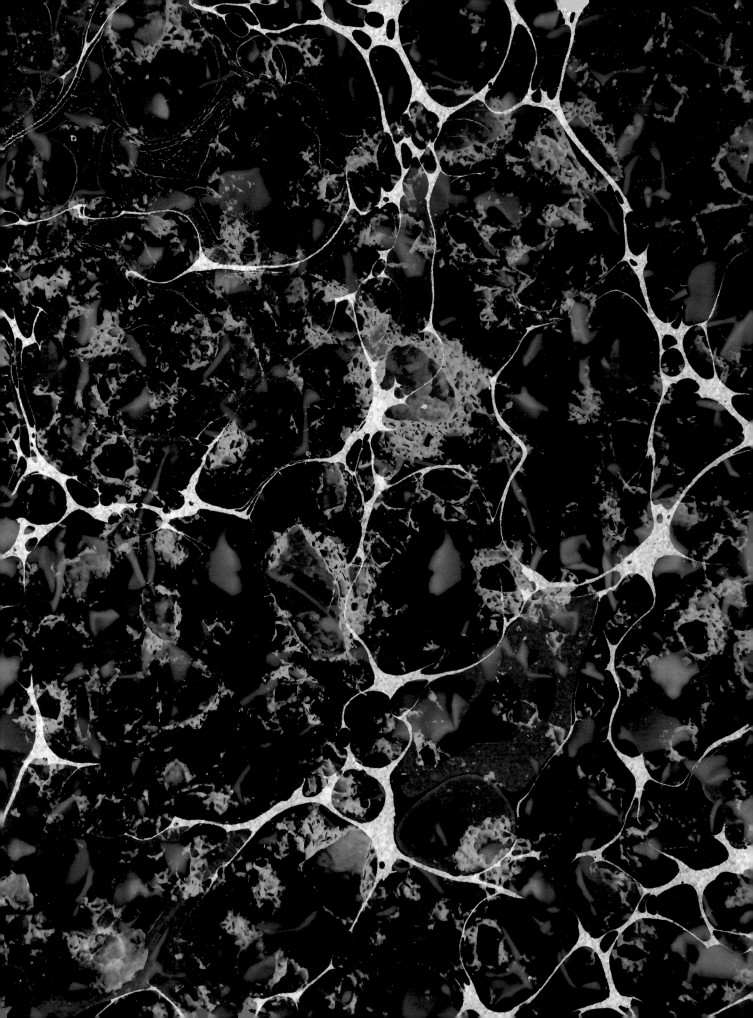

05

'The patterns we mimic are just as much in us as in the other parts of nature'

↪ **Leif Podhajsky**

Sentimental Layer, 2017

08

08

Summer Flower, 2019

09 →

Winter Flower, 2019

11

Wanderer At The Edge Of Time, 2011

Psychonaut, 2011

Lake McKay, 2018

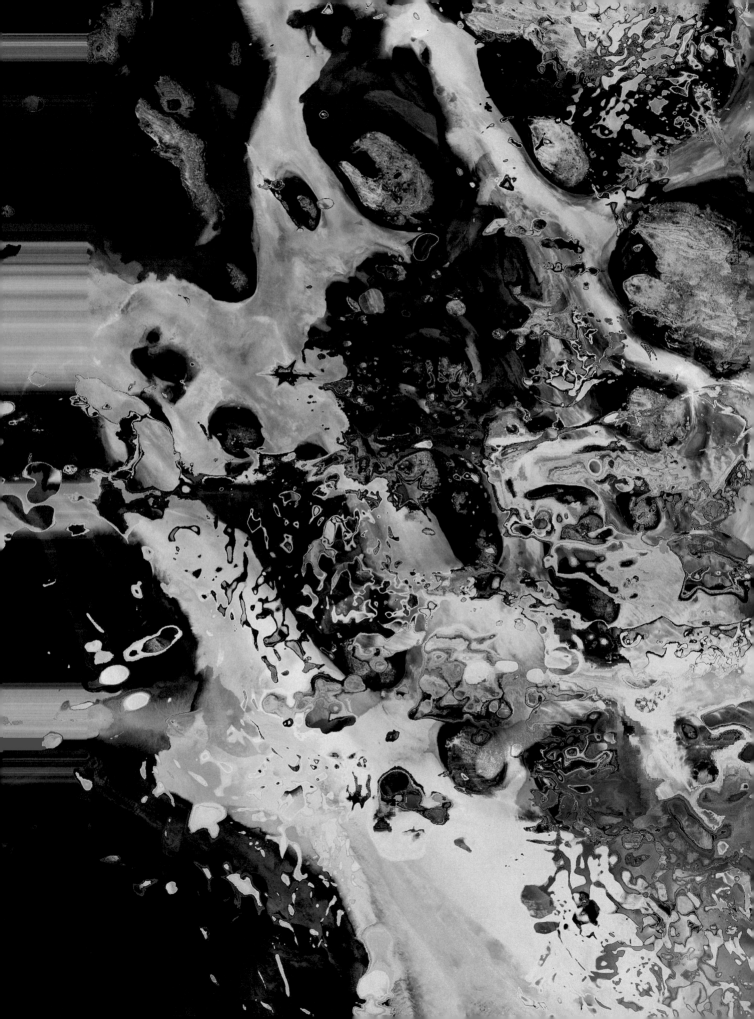

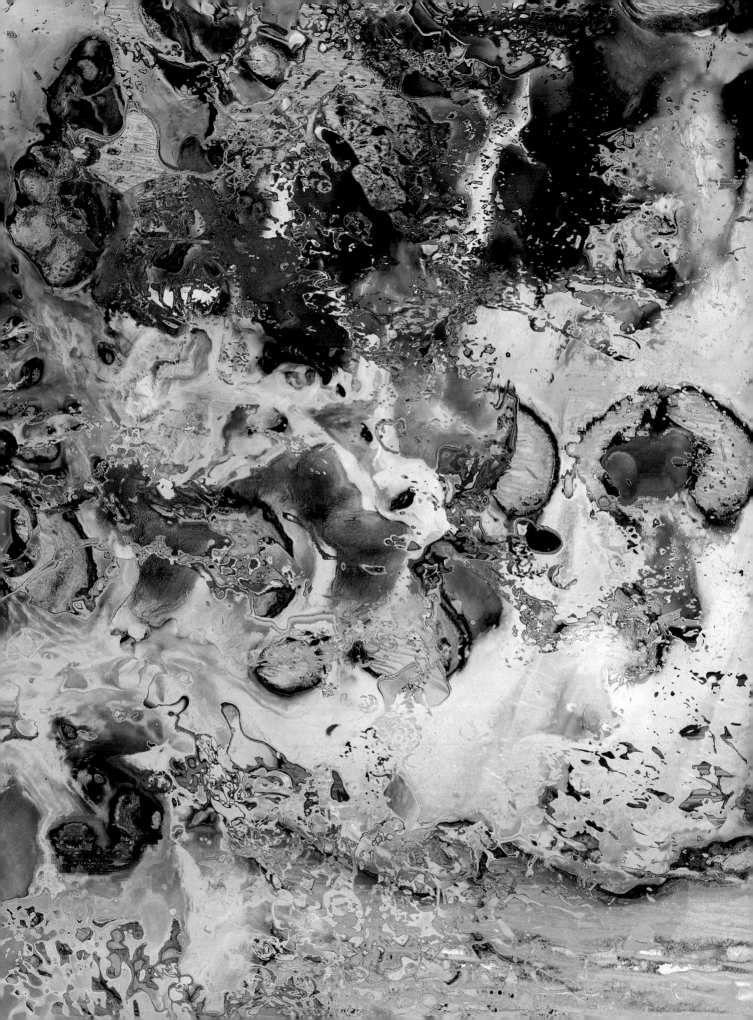

'For those who have grown up surrounded by nature ... it's hard to shake the yearning to return to it. Podhajsky constantly reminds himself of nature's importance, and his artwork reflects this'

Macro Gesture, 2016

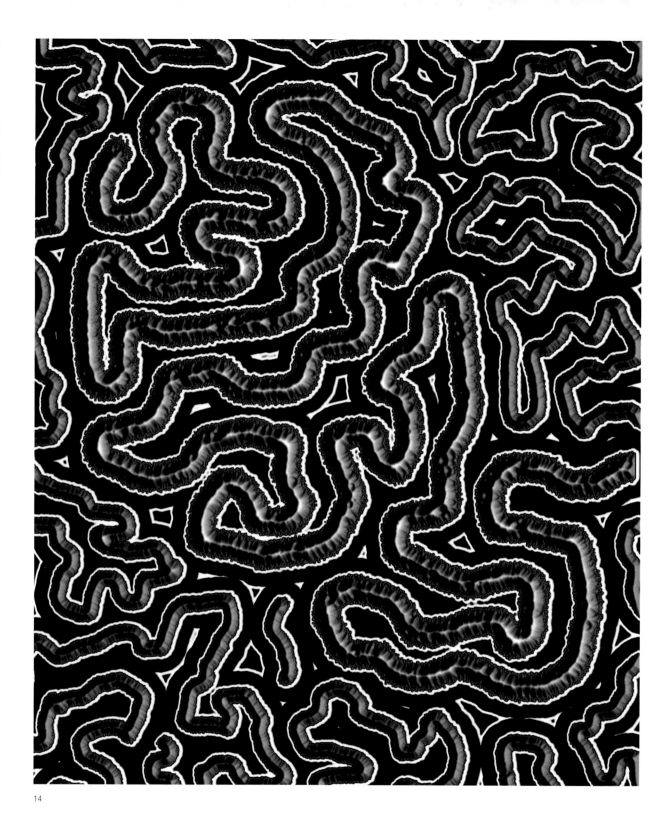

14

14

Earth Worm, 2018

15 →

Dark Matter, 2018

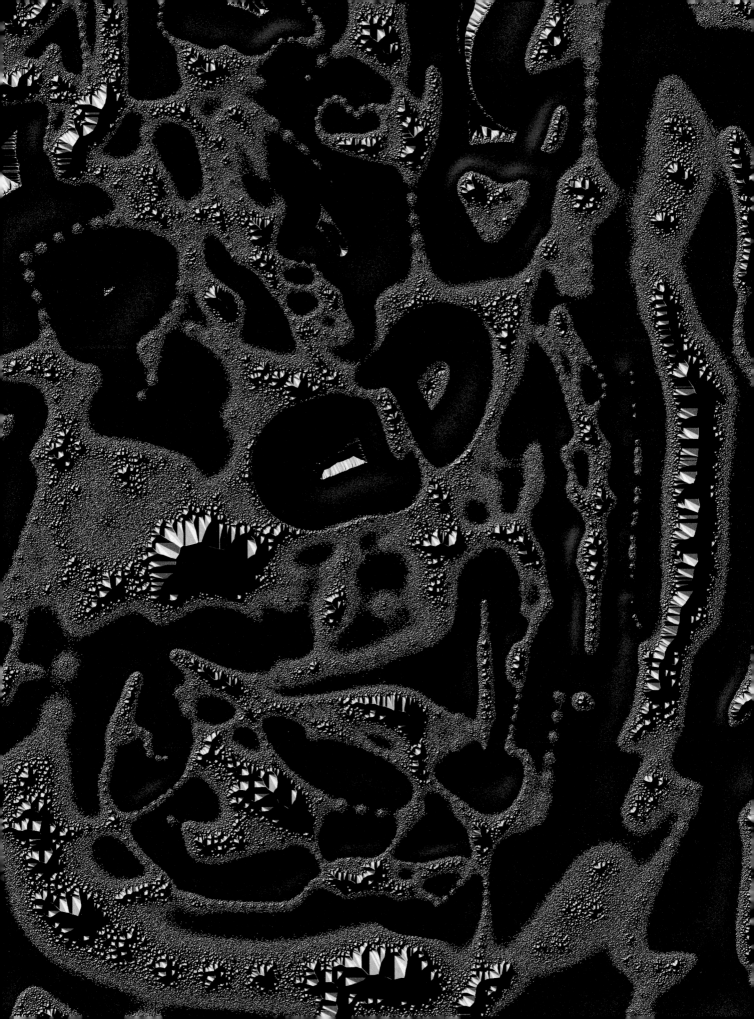

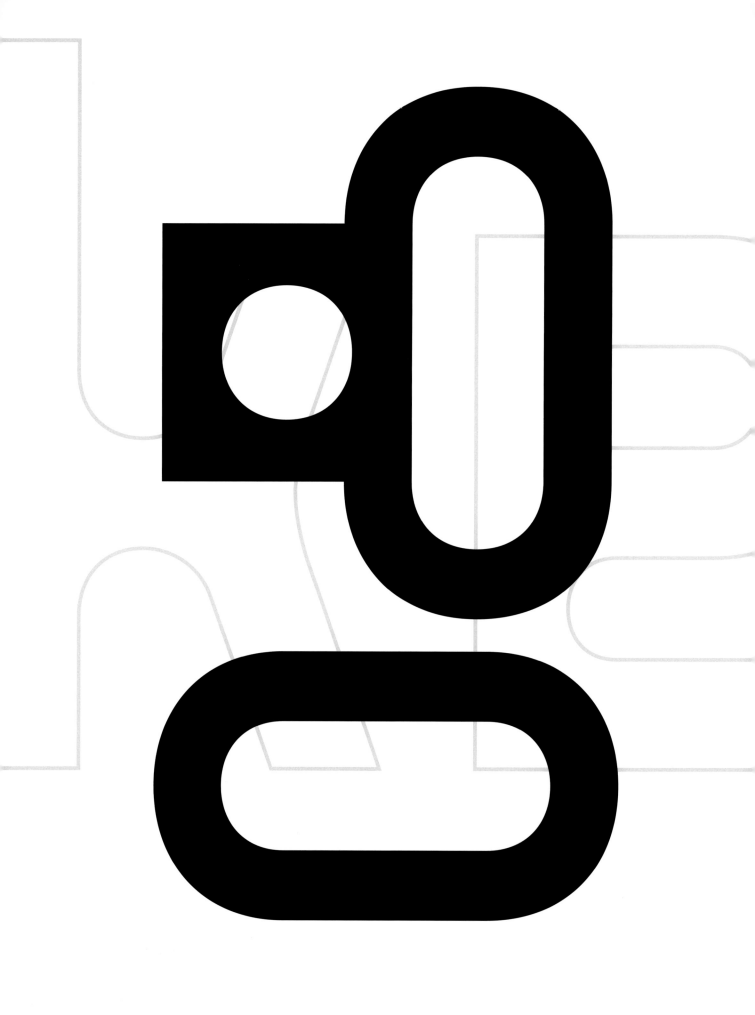

Lykke Li

WOUNDED RHYMES

[2011]

ATLANTIC RECORDS

/ ATUK109 / LC14666

I worked closely with Lykke and initially with David Girhammar, her creative partner. We spoke on Skype most mornings, orchestrating different approaches that Lykke wanted to explore. I then went to New York to finalize the album cover with Lykke; it was only the second or third cover I had ever created, so it was amazing to be able to go and meet with the artist.

I had a hotel in Midtown, but ended up crashing at a friend's a lot, which happened to be on the same street as Lykke was staying (at Peter's from Peter Bjorn and John). I would walk over in the morning with a bagel and coffee, and Lykke and I would discuss things before she'd zip off to meetings.

We decided that the duality of the black and white helped to reflect both a mysterious darkness and an emotional vulnerability, and added weight to the intimate heartache and emotional range that *Wounded Rhymes* covers.

↪ **Leif Podhajsky**

'[T]he duality of the black and white helped to reflect both a mysterious darkness and an emotional vulnerability'

↪ **Leif Podhajsky**

LYKKE LI   WOUNDED RHYMES

01

01

TITLE: *WOUNDED RHYMES*

YEAR: 2011

WORK TYPE: ALBUM ARTWORK

CLIENT: ATLANTIC RECORDS, LL RECORDINGS

MEDIUM: 12" GATEFOLD VINYL, CD, DIGITAL

02

02
Wounded Rhymes 12" vinyl package

→

03
Poster artwork for *Wounded Rhymes*

04

04

TITLE: 'SADNESS IS A BLESSING'

YEAR: 2011

WORK TYPE: SINGLE ARTWORK

CLIENT: ATLANTIC RECORDS, LL RECORDINGS

MEDIUM: DIGITAL

The dark monochromatic palette of the artwork was used as a direct reflection of the dark, intimate and personal themes in the music. There's an element of mystery and veiled darkness in the photography, which contrasts with the intimate layering of scratch marks, hand-set typography and little nuances which reveal Lykke at her most open and emotional.

↪ **Leif Podhajsky**

05

<u>TITLE</u>: 'I FOLLOW RIVERS'

<u>YEAR</u>: 2011

<u>WORK TYPE</u>: SINGLE ARTWORK

<u>CLIENT</u>: ATLANTIC RECORDS, LL RECORDINGS

<u>MEDIUM</u>: DIGITAL

05

09

Duke Dumont

DUALITY

[2020]

VIRGIN / EMI

/ V 3243 / CDV 3243

01

01

TITLE: *DUALITY*

YEAR: 2020

WORK TYPE: ALBUM ARTWORK

CLIENT: VIRGIN/EMI

MEDIUM: 2 x 12" VINYL, CD, DIGITAL

I wanted to create a world for the *Duality* album campaign that lived in both the darkness and the light. I think the music on the album really represents both sides: there are dark moments, but it's uplifting in equal measure. Taking the accepted dualities of good and evil, dark and light, the music to me walks the line between the two.

For the album cover we played with the ideas of the infinite, represented as black and punctuated by white strings. There is something in the distrupted lines that feels like a visual representation of sound patterns.

↳ **Leif Podhajsky**

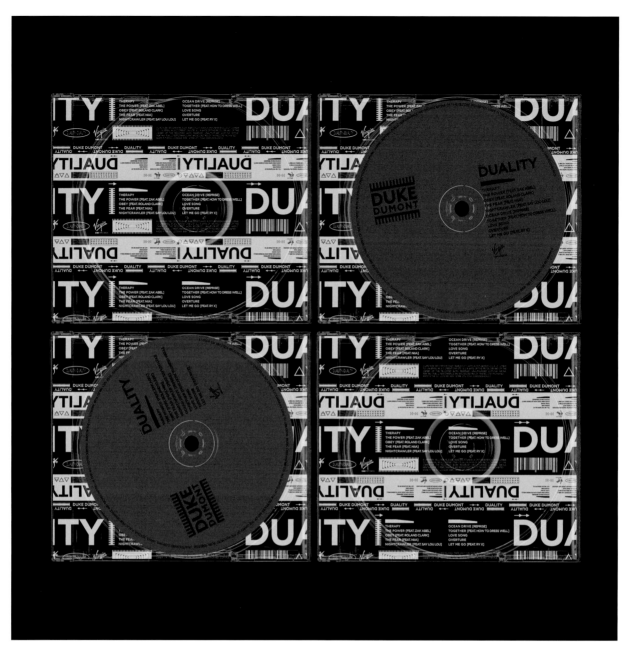

02

02
Duality CD label and inner-case artwork

03
Duality concert poster

DUKE DUMONT LIVE ▷◁▷◁▷ ◉

LA
LOS ANGELES

→→ DUKE **DUMONT** →→ LIVE

MAY-08

SHRINE EXPO HALL

PLUS SPECIAL **GUESTS**

Duke Dumont **LIVE**
May 08 – [Shrine Expo Hall]

Tick
DUMONT.COM

TICKETS DUKEDUMONT.COM TICKETS

2020 GOLDENVOICE

03

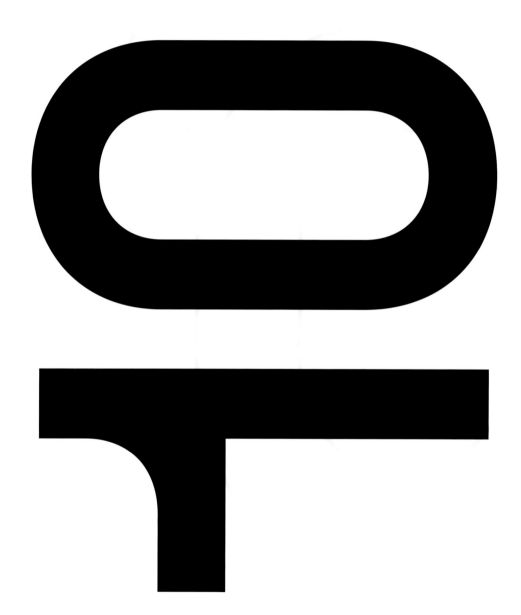

Young Magic

MELT
YOU WITH AIR
NIGHT IN THE OCEAN

[2011–2012]

CARPARK RECORDS

/ CAK 72
/ CAK 58
/ CAK 69

We were all in different parts of the world recording; it felt loose and chaotic. Melati in New York, Michael travelling in Argentina and Brazil, myself in Europe, the UK and eventually rural Mexico. A large part of this album was made in that house high up in the mountains above El Tepozteco. At the beginning of 2011 we met back up in New York and rented an old warehouse. I think we paid $300 each per month. It was above an illegal club, so when they closed during the weeknights, we would sneak down and use their sound system to listen to what we'd made. This became *Melt*.

Personally, that time felt very open-ended and fluid, as if the world was shapeshifting. This sounds absurd to say, of course, but it was a surreal year, a period when it felt like you were definitely in the stream, rather than watching the river.

And it was no doubt a time of immense change. Melati and I had just met. We were brimming with ideas and, I think, looking back, we seemed to share some kind of desire to dismantle and recreate our world. I'd sold everything I owned and bought a one-way ticket to Berlin with almost no money. Melati had done that a few years prior to New York. It wasn't ever easy, by any means, but we were a bit naive and the world seemed widescreen.

Technically, it was also the first time we had properly used a digital tool – the computer – for music making. The process felt open with possibilities, mirroring the mood of our world at the time. It was also portable, which we found liberating, having both come from backgrounds of making music in more traditional ways that required being tied to a physical location. The first song we ever recorded together on a laptop is the first song on *Melt*. In that way, for better or worse, our learning process was very public from the beginning; our interior landscape became an external one.

I visited Leif's studio one day to sit in on the process, and I remember him making a series of very slight, fluid edits with colour and tone, or warping the image dramatically with broad brushstrokes, yet the essence of the original image you'd first imagined remained. A figure between worlds. It was exploratory, searching, yet somehow still very assured and all-encompassing, like it had been there forever. The image perfectly encapsulated our thoughts around the album at the time. There was a sense that we were moving towards a new era where the world was crudely melding together, for better or worse. A new hyper-connectivity.

↪ **Isaac Emmanuel, Young Magic**

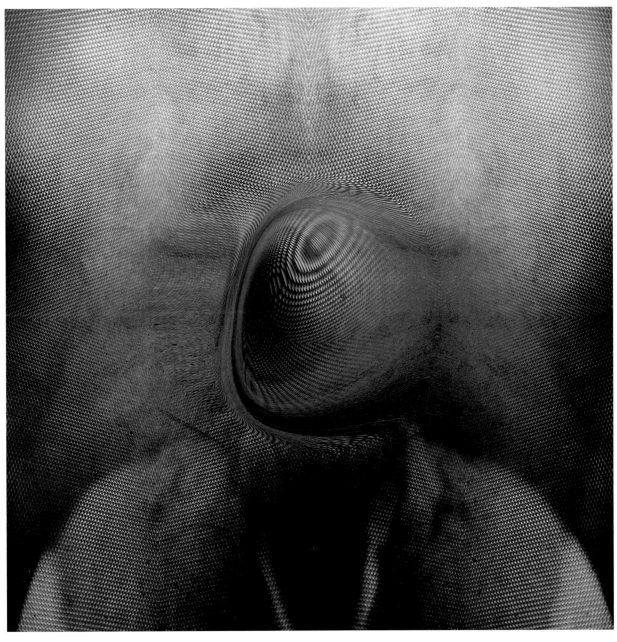

01

01 | 02

TITLE: *MELT*

YEAR: 2012

WORK TYPE: ALBUM ARTWORK

CLIENT: CARPARK RECORDS

MEDIUM: 12" VINYL, CD, DIGITAL, CASSETTE

02

03

03

TITLE: 'YOU WITH AIR' / 'SPARKLY'

YEAR: 2011

WORK TYPE: SINGLE ARTWORK

CLIENT: CARPARK RECORDS

MEDIUM: 7" VINYL, DIGITAL

I think there was this sense in everyone in our immediate circle that the world was sort of opening up very rapidly, and everyone was pushing a bit further: beyond their previous lives. I mean that in many respects, of course: geographically, obviously, but also in terms of some exploration around psychoactive plants and healing. It's interesting to see these conversations permeating the mainstream recently. At the same time, there was also this renewed interest in nature and we were spending more time in those spaces, which after living in cities for a while, was perhaps a catalyst in shifting priorities.

↪ **Isaac Emmanuel, Young Magic**

TITLE: 'NIGHT IN THE OCEAN' / 'SLIP TIME'

YEAR: 2011

WORK TYPE: SINGLE ARTWORK

CLIENT: CARPARK RECORDS

MEDIUM: 7" VINYL, DIGITAL

I remember we'd been having these very light-hearted discussions about the environmental crisis, how growth in technology might eventually intermesh with biology, and so on. Leif was clearly a gifted artist, and I remember sending him some early recordings we'd been working on and he immediately understood how it could be translated into a visual language. It's rare to find that type of innate understanding

↪ **Isaac Emmanuel, Young Magic**

Crooked Colours

LANGATA

[2019]

SWEAT IT OUT

/ SWEATA019V / SWEATA014

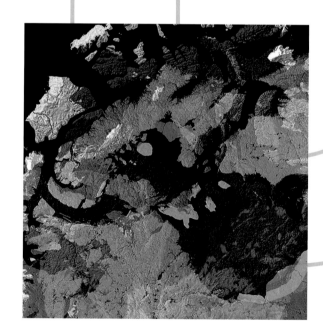

CROOKED COLOURS
LANGATA.

A		B	
	Tappy		Langata
	I'll Be There		Spacial
	Do It Like You		Snow
	Heart String		Lose Someone
	Hold On		Shadow

01

01

TITLE: *LANGATA*

YEAR: 2019

WORK TYPE: ALBUM ARTWORK

CLIENT: SWEAT IT OUT

MEDIUM: 12" VINYL, CD, DIGITAL

I wanted this cover to feel like an old topographical map of an unknown place; it has the feeling of looking down from a satellite on to a lava field of colours, with little fjords and islands forking out into the blackness of space. A representation of the world that the songs on the album create.

↳ **Leif Podhajsky**

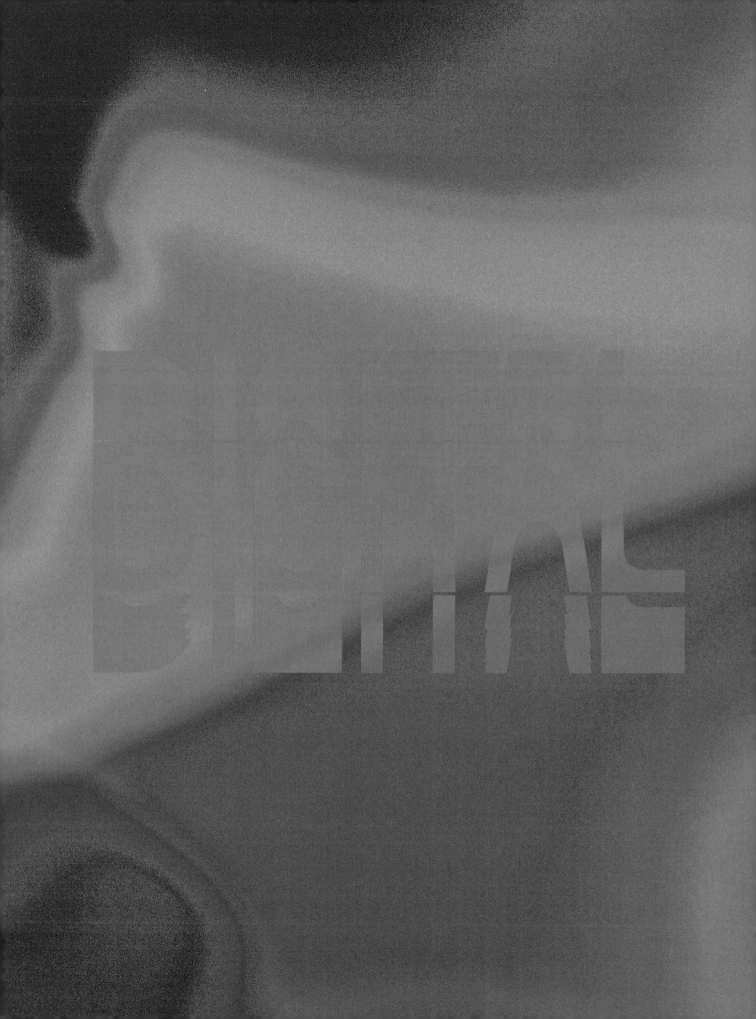

Digital Ritual → ◇

Our modern understanding of the word 'ritual' has two sides. In the spiritual and more traditional sense, a ritual refers to a ceremony that marks a certain rite of passage – a point of change or transition in a life, such as being born, becoming an adult or dying. Today, though, the word has assumed another, quite opposite meaning to fit with a narrative of consumption. Advertising not only draws on the symbolism that comes from ritual, but it has also absorbed the word 'ritual' into its language and changed its meaning. Consumer rituals are aligned with consistency and habit – cosmetic rituals, daily-coffee rituals, social-media-posting rituals. The rituals of consumption embrace the flow and comfort of repetition, whereas 'ritual' in the traditional sense marks a temporary ceremonial departure from those very things. Repeated behaviours are revered above the rituals linked to rites of passage in our natural lives. Predictable behaviour has a high value in a capitalist system.

As Michael Pollan puts it: 'Habits are undeniably useful tools, relieving us of the need to run a complex mental operation every time we're confronted with a new task or situation. Yet they also relieve us of the need to stay awake to the world: to attend, feel, think, and then act in a deliberate manner. (That is, from freedom rather than compulsion.)'[1] In his book *How to Change Your Mind*, he advocates for the ability of psychedelic drugs to give us a perspective outside of the accepted structures of society, which become more and more ingrained in us as we get older. As Pollan sees it, habits are integral to our function as human beings on a day-to-day basis – but do we get enough opportunities to 'break out' of these patterns every so often? Podhajsky meanwhile notes that 'with psychedelics, the experience is confrontational, liberating and interesting. It gets rid of the ego.'

The mind becomes conditioned to the repetitive habits of the commuter's week. During the daily journey to work, like a sleepwalker, the body takes itself to the same place on the platform and arrives at the same café counter, day in and day out, to chant 'an Americano with cold oat milk, please'. Structure and routine keep us comfortable and enable us to function, but there is something to be said for the disintegration of structure once in a while. Gillian Tett calls liminality – meaning a state of transition or the start of something new – 'the cultural equivalent of the pupation that insects undergo: patterns become untethered and fluid, to be remoulded'.[2] The word *limen* literally means 'doorway' or 'threshold' and, to use Aldous Huxley's term, perhaps by journeying through the 'Door in the Wall'[3] there is a way to find an outside perspective, free from the complex networks of habits and repetitions of modern life. As Podhajsky says, in order to be creative there is a need 'to keep the momentum of new experience'.

Looking back 5,000 years to the Neolithic period, there is evidence to suggest that monuments such as the famous Stonehenge in Wiltshire (see F3) were divided into stone-built and wood-built circular structures according to use – ritual/sacred, or social. Stone represented the 'sacred', and is often surrounded by physical, liminal boundaries to

F1

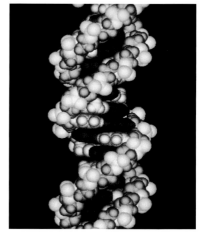

F2

F1
Detail of an internet map showing complex networks

F2
Digitally generated DNA molecule created by the National Cancer Institute

F3
Computer rendering of the Neolithic ritual site Stonehenge in Wiltshire

delineate it from wooden structures, which represented the 'social' environment. Signs of feasting and the bones of domesticated animals were found at the wooden henges, while stone henges were 'clean' and had none of the same signs of use. Now, for a lot of non-spiritual people, the divide between sacred and social is tied to the act of earning money and then spending it – delineated by the workplace, with its rules and 'ceremonial' dress, and the non-workplace, with the weekend harbouring a sense of release. What's more, our social 'spaces' have moved away from being tangible physical environments and towards digital platforms and social media.

'Rushing mountain streams were rerouted to create an artificial watercourse that echoed through the tunnels; conch trumpet shells have been found, and fragments of anthracite mirror that may have bounced light through the galleries along with sound.'[4] Humans have shaped and controlled their surroundings in order to heighten sensory experience for thousands of years, as cultural historian Mike Jay describes here in his account of an early archaeological site discovered in the Andes. Sound and light are part of the pathway to altered experience. Evidence suggests that the most sacred areas in dwellings or ritual sites incidentally have the highest levels of hertz – the most echoey part of a cave, for instance, where the greater frequency of sound waves can cause vibrations that have a physical effect on the body.

Podhajsky describes music as 'a transportation device, it can transcend time and space'. We forget the ritualistic properties of music – the fact that music, in general, has a combination of elements that grow into an intangible recipe for making us feel things. Yes, there are drugs, but not all psychedelic stimulation comes from dropping a pill – it can also come from and be heightened by sound combined with a specially constructed atmosphere of lights, rhythm and moving bodies in a club or at a gig, just like the Andean ritual site described by Jay. Today, the temporally spaced out and widely celebrated rituals such as passing into a new year have become condensed and more frequent. The lack of time for reflection in the working week speeds people into the weekend with a need to decompress, to dance away the tension from the bodies that have been sitting in front of computers like loaded springs – bodies that are built to trawl landscapes for food, to move, to be used.

Philosopher Jaron Lanier says: 'We miss the wilds. But they scare us. We hate the city, which jams us in with aliens. But we need it. So we fake the wilds in a city without an apparent center. We are drawn in by the feeling, but the actuality is that we become beholden to new centers that exploit us. We have yet to settle into a comfortable shape.'[5]

Lanier writes about the concept of the public square in the digital age. In our huge cities and cavernous digital social spaces, we are centreless – without a particular gathering space or sense of boundary. Information has become increasingly sourceless, repeated and reused endlessly, echoing through the halls of the internet. Online communities create their own runic languages composed of digital symbols, emojis, GIFs and memes, which are then recycled by corporations to create the

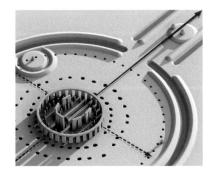

F3

perfect marketing algorithms and collect data. As Lanier says, '[f]reedom is more fleeting in the digital domain than in physicality. Bulldozers can trample an ancient city and impose the designs of a careless new empire.'[6] Perhaps we are moving further away from the source of things. Although, sometimes it is fun to jump headfirst down the rabbit hole of information that is the internet: 'I love that treasure hunt,' Podhajsky admits.

In the age of social media, we are not only placing ourselves at a remove from the source of the information we absorb. We are also able to view ourselves as individuals at that point of remove, to present and perceive ourselves constantly through digital media. If psychedelics help to 'get rid of ego', then social media platforms nurture it and help it to grow. The development of artificial intelligence is part of this bid to further perceive and recreate the self. In some strange way AI could be said to be an attempt at 'mind-manifesting', trying to hold up a mirror to the human mind by attempting to recreate it. The Google Deep Dream Generator (see F5) is an example of AI developed to mimic the associative and creative processes of the human mind. The software 'creates' artworks derived from an original photograph, remaking 'an image to include whatever it is being told to see in the image. The end result is a hallucination of the image that has a psychedelic look.'[7]

Adam Curtis's 2011 documentary *All Watched Over by Machines of Loving Grace*, untangles the ideology, beginning in the 1950s and continuing through the dawn of the digital age, where nature was said to be ordered into 'ecosystems' just like electrical-circuit-based computer systems. By contrast, AI experiments such as Google's Deep Dream 'hallucinations' and algorithms are striving to replicate and understand the chaotic nature of the human mind and, in turn, the chaos of digital platforms that tirelessly try to cater for, manipulate and interfere with its needs. Do we want an algorithm to apply artificial structure to our chaotic natures, or should we work to reinstate rituals that accurately reflect milestones in our lives and move us forward creatively?

'Almost everything in modern life can be a hindrance! Taxes, which washing machine liquid to buy, Instagram … Society is set up in a way to make it difficult to be creative. It's why a lot of creative people (which really is everyone) feel at odds with how the world works. I think there should be a much higher emphasis put on creativity and the exploration of ideas. As someone who works creatively day to day I have taught myself ways to tap into this space. For me music, nature, calmness and boredom all help me get back to that space. The problem can be switching back again; I'd much rather live in that creative sphere, but in the end one doesn't exist without the other. We get hungry, tired and drawn back to our bodies and in turn loosen the connection with the creative realm. The challenge is exercising these rituals that make it easier to flow between the two states as seamlessly as possible. Which is not always an easy thing. It's a constant battle and one in which society offers no support.

F4
Aerial photograph of La Plata, the capital city of Buenos Aires Province in Argentina. La Plata is a planned city, designed in the 1880s to sit within a perfect square

F5
A photograph of jellyfish, manipulated by Google's Deep Dream generator

F6
Leif Podhajsky and friends pictured during a 'Psych Hike' trip to Scotland

F4

F5

F6

'We are all creative people; I think that some have just learned how to use it better than others among all the chaos.'

Leif Podhajsky

It seems as though a kind of constraint informed by experiences of breaking with structure – such as altered states or psychedelic trips – can help to nurture the creative process. Podhajsky says having a variety of constraints sometimes leads to his best work. For example, in the process of creating album art there is the consideration of how the work will be perceived by the audience you are trying to connect with. 'There are all the different platforms and sizes for the work, defined by the constraints of the music world. The label, the band, me – all these different inputs might change the direction quite a lot.' Sometimes the endlessness of the information at our fingertips inhibits our freedom to choose what we engage with. We are left with what is curated for us, and it is easy to be drip-fed our knowledge by algorithms.

When Podhajsky moved to London, a desire to meet new people and escape the constraints of technology and the city drove him to join a hiking group. 'Eventually it morphed into a different beast. This thirst for nature while living in a city was evident in a lot of people. Not only for nature, but for a connection with each other, and a deeper connection to everything started to develop. A new group had formed (and still runs to this day) with the very tongue-in-cheek name "Psych Hike". A few times a year myself and close friends will rent a remote house, castle or cabin and get together away from all the noise, make good food, hike and take mushrooms or truffles. For me it's really important to not only keep the connection with my friends alive but also re-establish the link with nature and ourselves. It's activities like these that I think are important for everyone; it can be a really good way to reset and actually have some space to think about what is important. A sort of modern ritual.'

1. Michael Pollan, *How to Change Your Mind: The New Science of Psychedelics*, Penguin (2018), page 15
2. Gillian Tett, 'How ancient rituals help us adapt to the digital age', *Financial Times*, https://www.ft.com/content/c3a55ae0-9797-11e9-9573-ee5cbb98ed36 [accessed 21 July 2020]
3. Aldous Huxley, *The Doors of Perception*, Vintage (2004, first published 1954), page 50
4. Mike Jay, *Mescaline: A Global History of the First Psychedelic*, Yale University Press (2019), page 23
5. Jaron Lanier, 'What Makes the Public Square Square?', *The Future of Public Space: SOM Thinkers Series*, Metropolis Books (2018), page 42
6. Lanier, ibid.
7. Matt MacFarland, 'Google's psychedelic "paint brush" raises the oldest question in art', *The Washington Post*, 10 March 2016, https://www.washingtonpost.com/news/innovations/wp/2016/03/10/googles-psychedelic-paint-brush-raises-the-oldest-question-in-art/ [accessed 21 July 2020]

'We are all creative people; I think that some have just learned how to use it better than others among all the chaos'

↪ Leif Podhajsky

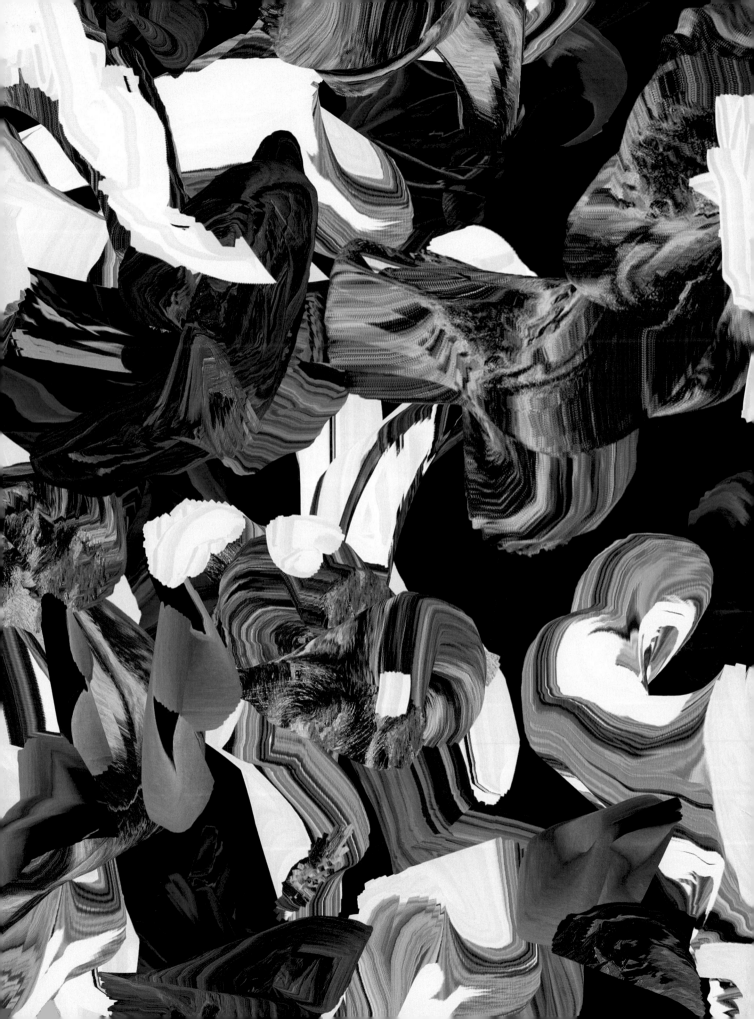

'With psychedelics, the experience is confrontational, liberating and interesting. It gets rid of the ego'

↪ **Leif Podhajsky**

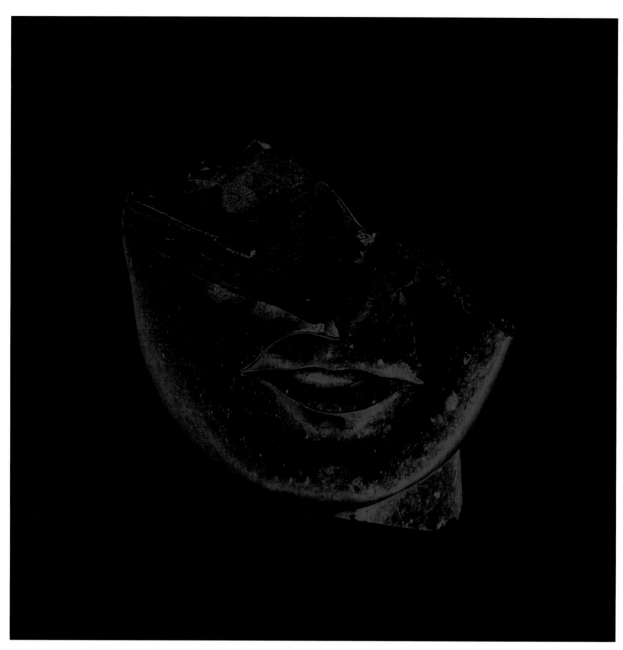

03

06

06

The Syntactical Nature Of Reality, 2016

07 ⟶

Main Lake, 2016

'This thirst for nature while living in a city was evident in a lot of people. Not only for nature, but for a connection with each other'

↪ Leif Podhajsky

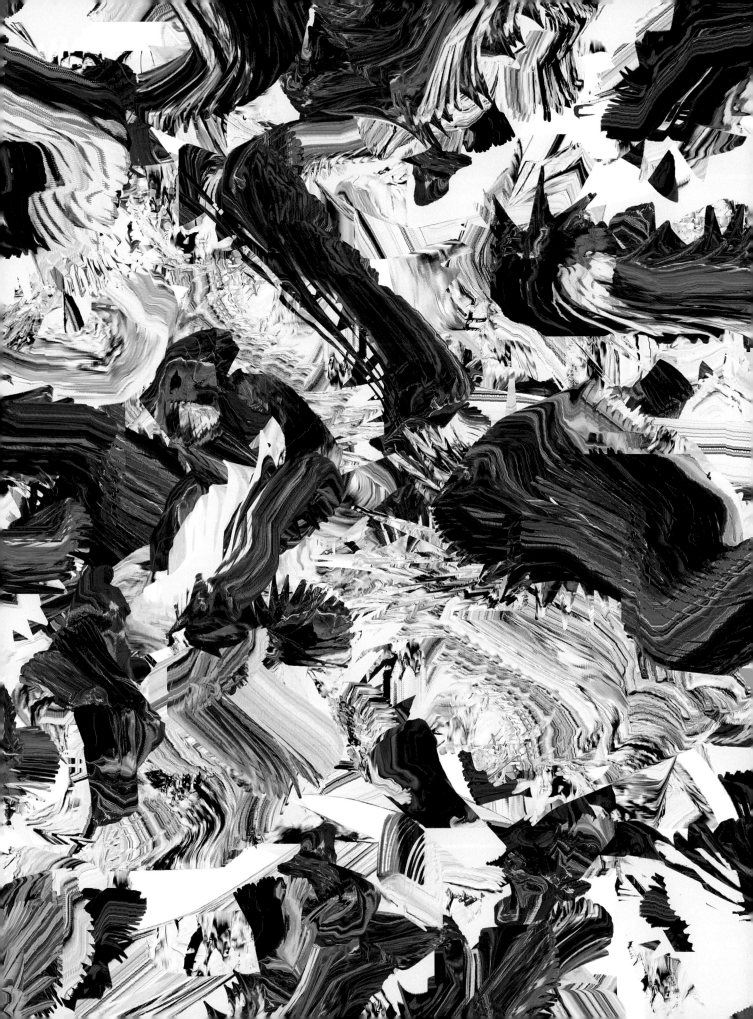

09

09

Paointss, 2020

10 →

Saetrty Reprise, 2018

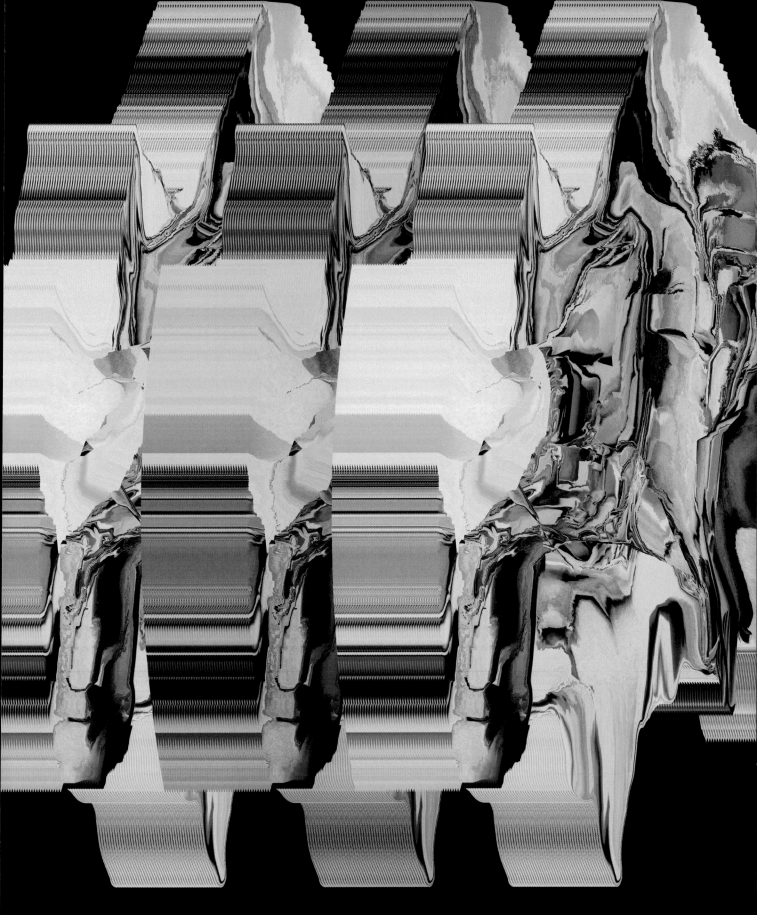

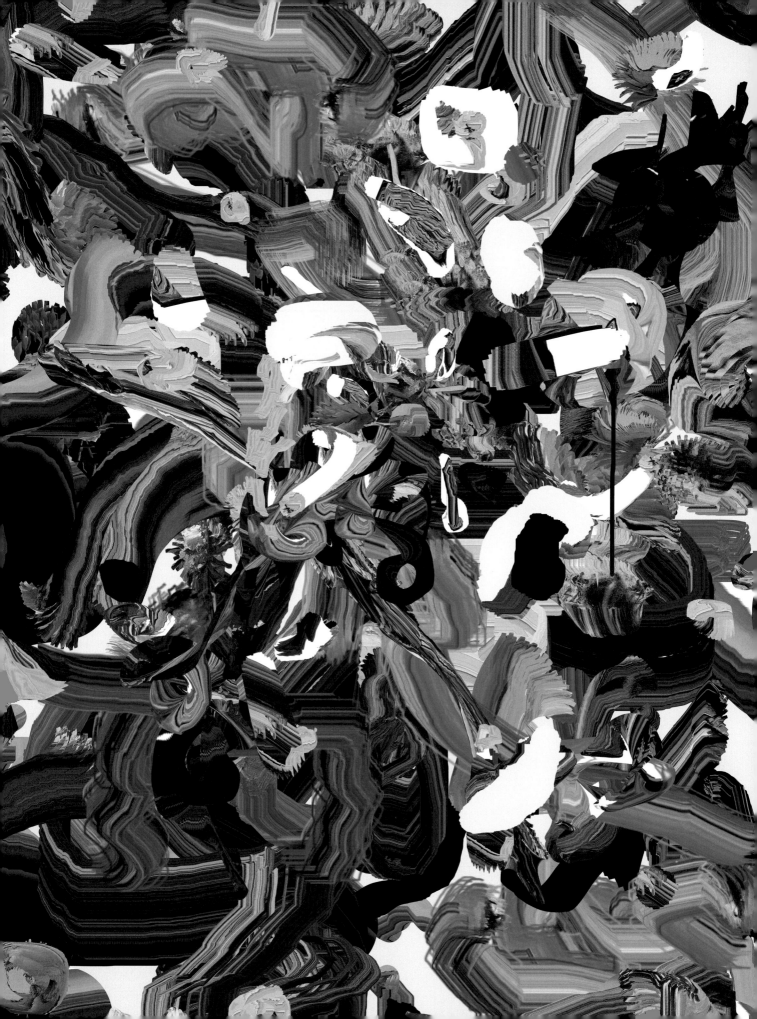

12

← 11
Untitled, 2020

12
Untitled II, 2020

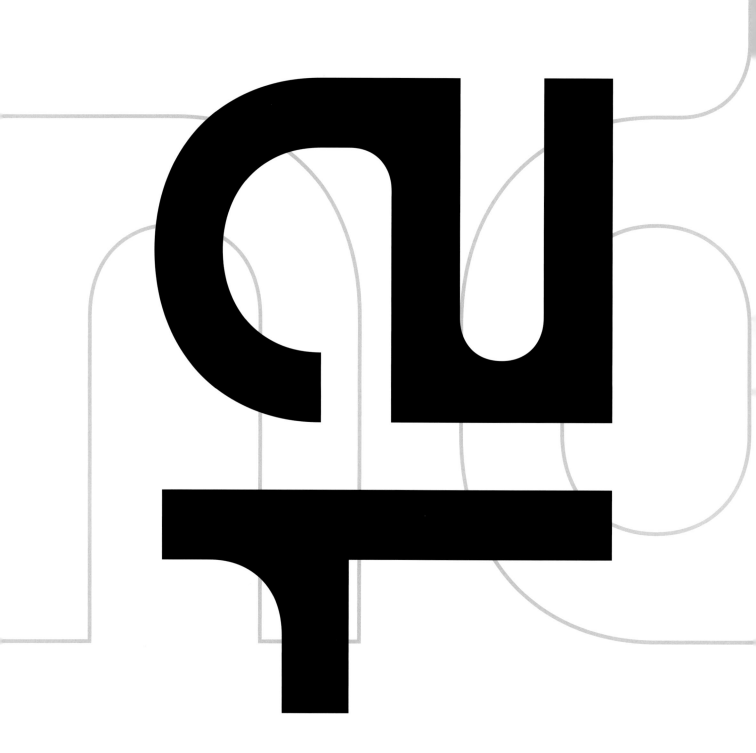

London Grammar

TRUTH IS A BEAUTIFUL THING

[2017]

MINISTRY OF SOUND

/ MADART2LTD / MADART2

London Grammar came to my studio a few times, and we chatted about the themes and ideas on the new album, what they'd gone through personally and emotionally writing it. There's this sense of raw emotion and darkness on the album, but with a lightness shining through. They really wanted to delve into the human condition through natural landscapes, a place set between dreams and reality.

The band had showed me some old films and album covers that had this raw, un-digital feel, sort of an ode to the past but also pushing into the future. So for the singles we led with shots of the band, but then for the album we shifted the attention to them as individuals: close up, more candid. Set with a black background, as if they were coming out of the dark into light. The album photo has a beautiful soft, warm quality and also a dark feel: this duality I think complements the set of songs on the album perfectly.

↪ Leif Podhajsky

'There's this sense of raw emotion and darkness on the album, but with a lightness shining through'

↪ Leif Podhajsky

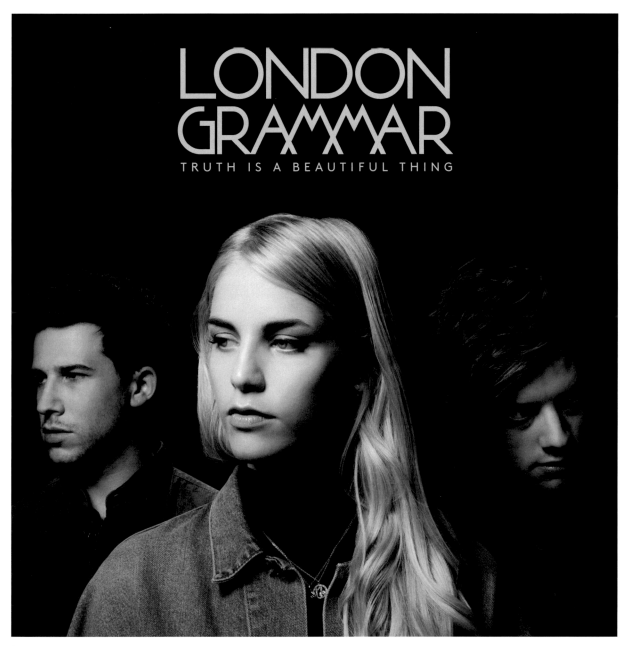

01

01

TITLE: *TRUTH IS A BEAUTIFUL THING*

YEAR: 2017

WORK TYPE: ALBUM ARTWORK

CLIENT: MINISTRY OF SOUND

MEDIUM: 12" VINYL, CD, DIGITAL

02

03

02 | 03

The CD Digipak folds out to reveal a highly contrasted black-and-white desert landscape, adding weight to the 'light from dark' aspect of the themes on the cover. This is balanced with the warmer pinkish tones of the CDs and type that help to offset the darkness. – Leif Podhajsky

04

04

TITLE: 'OH WOMAN OH MAN'

YEAR: 2017

WORK TYPE: SINGLE ARTWORK

CLIENT: MINISTRY OF SOUND

MEDIUM: 7" VINYL, DIGITAL

I've always been a huge admirer of the German Romantic painter Caspar David Friedrich, with his depictions of landscapes featuring humans dwarfed by the power of nature. I thought this was a good starting point, and we set about coming up with a way to communicate these ideas in a campaign. We shot the band in the Californian desert with photographer Eliot Lee Hazel, setting them among enormous dunes and sun-drenched expanses that had a dreamy, almost otherworldly feel. Having the band so small in the midst of these vast landscapes helps convey the emotion and strength of the songs, – this balance between light and dark, but also a sense of something greater than ourselves.

↪ **Leif Podhajsky**

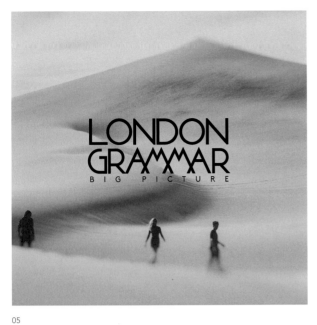

05

06

07

05

TITLE: 'BIG PICTURE'

YEAR: 2017

WORK TYPE: SINGLE ARTWORK

CLIENT: MINISTRY OF SOUND

MEDIUM: 7" VINYL, DIGITAL

06

TITLE: 'HELL TO THE LIARS'

YEAR: 2017

WORK TYPE: SINGLE ARTWORK

CLIENT: MINISTRY OF SOUND

MEDIUM: DIGITAL

07

TITLE: 'NON BELIEVER'

YEAR: 2017

WORK TYPE: SINGLE ARTWORK

CLIENT: MINISTRY OF SOUND

MEDIUM: DIGITAL

13

Nick Mulvey

WAKE UP NOW

[2017]

CAROLINE RECORDS

/ MULVEY013 / MULVEY014

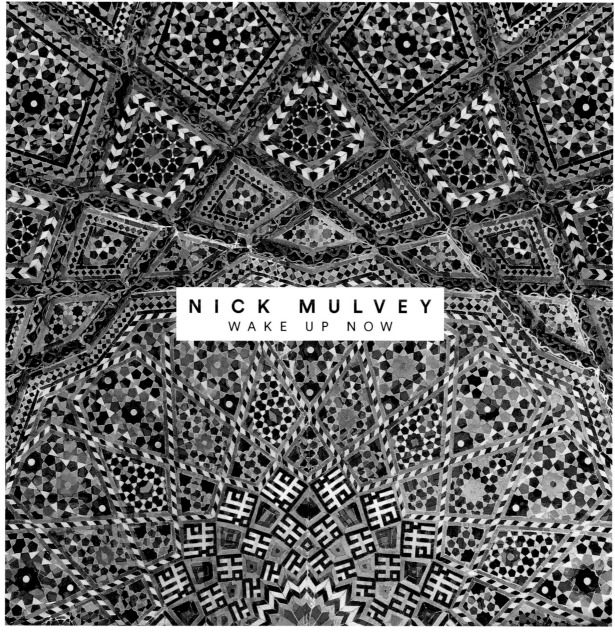

01

01

TITLE: *WAKE UP NOW*

YEAR: 2017

WORK TYPE: ALBUM ARTWORK

CLIENT: CAROLINE RECORDS

MEDIUM: 12" VINYL, CD, DIGITAL

Nick came to my studio one evening with a friend, and we discussed aspects of the album and what he wanted it to represent. I started just riffing with some images and ideas in Photoshop, which was an unusual way to work for me. We settled on some Arabic motifs I had been exploring. The original motif used in the final artwork is from the Nasir al-Mulk Mosque in Iran. We found a photographer in Iran who could go and take a photograph on location for us. I then set about altering the colours and overlaying other patterns to get the final album artwork.

↪ **Leif Podhajsky**

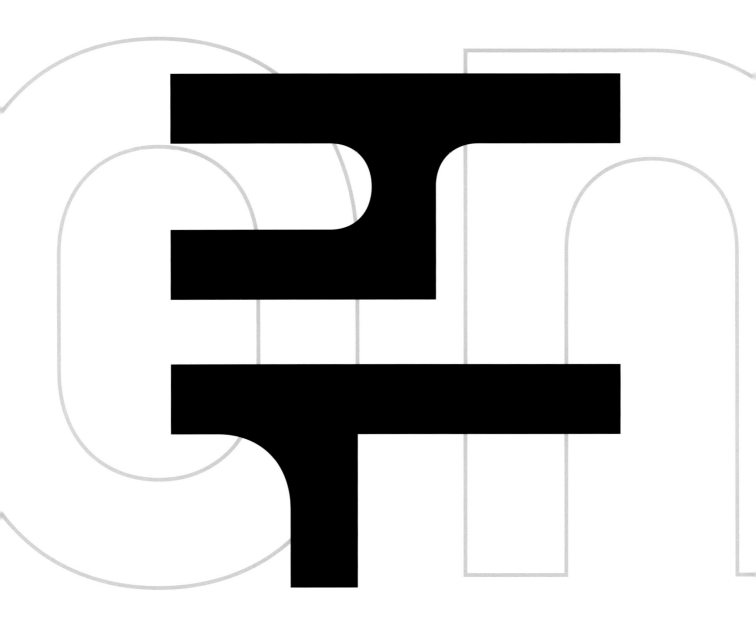

Of Monsters and Men

BENEATH THE SKIN

[2015]

REPUBLIC RECORDS

/ 472742-5 / 472850-1
/ B0023093-01 OX01

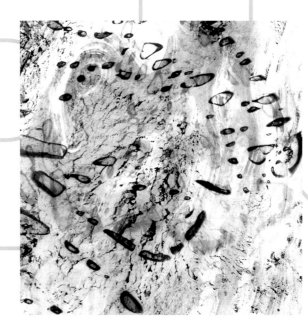

We wrote and recorded *Beneath the Skin* from 2014 to 2015. At that time we had been touring extensively for about two years following the success of our debut album. It was a totally new experience for us. Touring is fast, exciting, and every night you are rushed with adrenalin. You are surrounded by people. You feel like you wrote something for yourself and then you can literally see how it isn't yours any more. It's a feeling like no other.

Coming back home, to Iceland, you immediately noticed the stark difference. It felt like you had been moving at the speed of light and suddenly you were still. Like everyone was at a different tempo. It felt isolating, but a lot of great things happen when you are forced to spend time with yourself and figure yourself out.

Beneath the Skin is written in that headspace. Of coming back to the calm. But also trying to figure out where to go from here, and who we were as a band and individuals. It was a beautiful time. Making the album spanned many seasons, but the one I remember the most is winter. We recorded the album in the Icelandic studio Sundlaugin, an old swimming pool turned into a studio that used to belong to Sigur Rós, and finished it at our producer Rich Costey's studio in LA.

↪ **Nanna Bryndís Hilmarsdóttir, Of Monsters and Men**

'Coming back home, to Iceland, you immediately noticed the stark difference. It felt like you had been moving at the speed of light and suddenly you were still'

↪ **Nanna Bryndís Hilmarsdóttir, Of Monsters and Men**

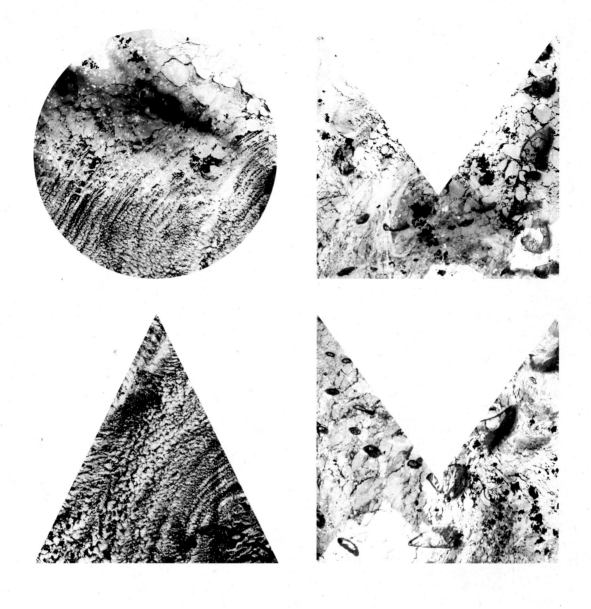

01

01

TITLE: *BENEATH THE SKIN*

YEAR: 2015

WORK TYPE: ALBUM ARTWORK

CLIENT: REPUBLIC RECORDS

MEDIUM: 2 × 12″ VINYL, CD, DIGITAL

02

Nature and our surroundings have had a huge impact on our songwriting. I think especially for *Beneath the Skin*, being at home in Iceland was such an inspiration. I feel so fortunate to have nature in the back yard. Whenever I feel stuck or low I know that seeing a mountain or the ocean will clear my head.

Sonically, we like to build our songs like landscapes and our lyrics are filled with references to nature.

We are surrounded by mountains, lava fields and ocean. It's impossible not to be affected.

I don't think we could have written the same kind of album if we were somewhere else in the world. You write about what you know, and at that time we were immersed in Iceland.

↳ **Nanna Bryndís Hilmarsdóttir, Of Monsters and Men**

02
Beneath the Skin 12" vinyl

→

03
A set of symbols created for the *Beneath the Skin* album

04

I think that the cover art is perfect for the album's atmosphere. The black and white landscape feels isolating and cold, but there's also this vastness and space in it.

For each song on the album, there is a symbol. Leif had the task of interpreting and designing each symbol with reference to the lyrics. This was such an interesting idea, because it gives each song an identity but also adds a mysterious layer to it.

Sometimes when a song has a special meaning to you but it isn't the single, you don't have as many opportunities to showcase the layers of the song. Making symbols just means that each song is a world on its own.

↪ **Nanna Bryndís Hilmarsdóttir, Of Monsters and Men**

OMAM

WOLVES WITHOUT
TEETH

05

06

06 | 07 | 08

TITLE: *BENEATH THE SKIN*

YEAR: 2015

WORK TYPE: BOX SET ARTWORK

CLIENT: REPUBLIC RECORDS

MEDIUM: 2 × 12" VINYL, BONUS 10" VINYL,

DIGITAL, POSTER

This package was nominated for a Grammy Award

07

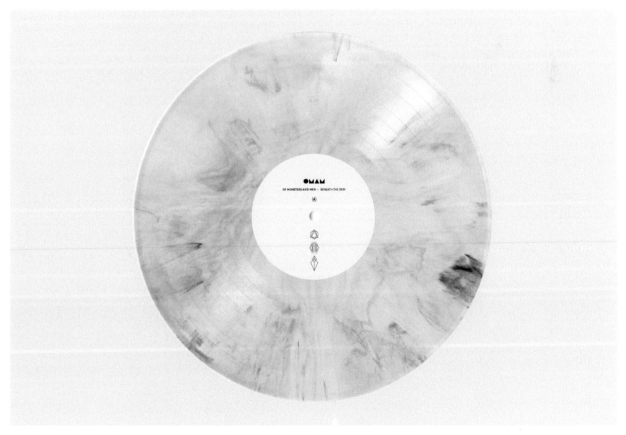

08

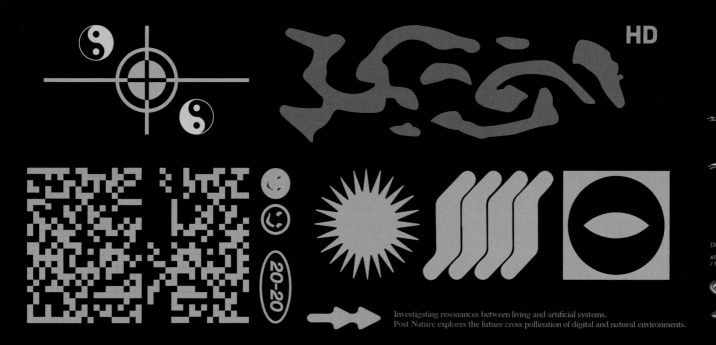

20-20

Investigating resonances between living and artificial systems.
Post Nature explores the future cross pollination of digital and natural environments.

[2020]
ATLANTIC RECORD
/ 1·526549 / 2·52...

	A	B
	ExtremeVisions	
	Sudden Action	
	True Vision	
	C	D
	Organic Digital	
	Digital Nature	
	Postnaturalism	

Anthropocene HD

POST NATURE EXPLORES THE ANTHROPOCENE AGE IN WHICH HUMAN ACTIVITY HAS BEEN THE DOMINANT INFLUENCE ON CLIMATE AND THE ENVIRONMENT. THIS ALTERING OF NATURE RESULTS IN NEW PERCEPTIONS OF WHAT NATURE IS AND HOW WE LIVE WITHIN THE NEW CONFINES OF A DAMAGED ECO-SYSTEM. POST NATURE EXPLORES THE ANTHROPOCENE AGE IN WHICH HUMAN ACTIVITY HAS BEEN THE DOMINANT INFLUENCE ON CLIMATE AND THE ENVIRONMENT. THIS ALTERING OF NATURE RESULTS IN NEW PERCEPTIONS OF WHAT NATURE IS AND HOW WE LIVE WITHIN THE NEW CONFINES OF A DAMAGED ECO-SYSTEM.

20-20

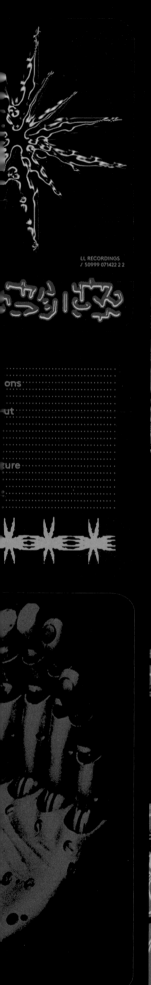

LL RECORDINGS
/ 50999 071422 2 2

ons

ut

ture

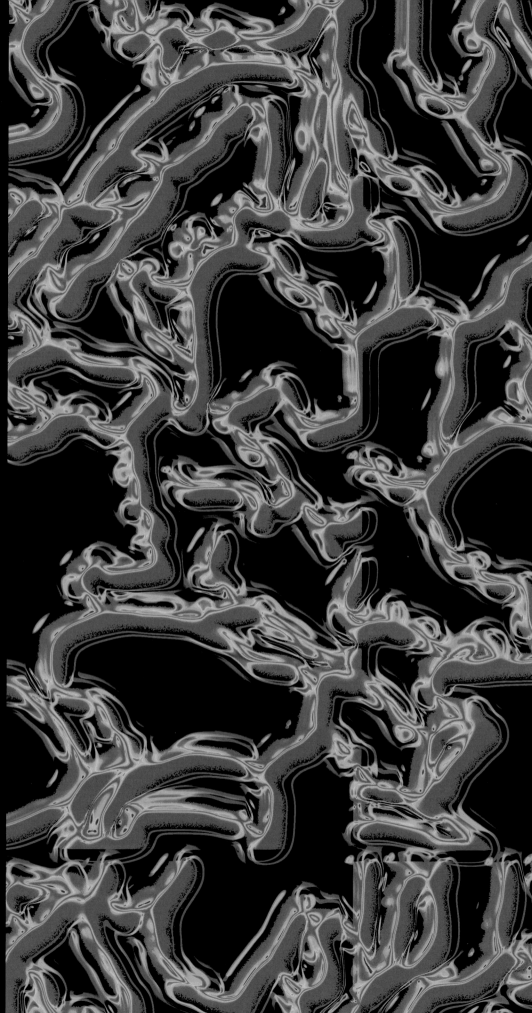

[2020]

184 – 211

THEME_04_ANTHROPOCENE
NEW-PSYCHEDELIA

Anthropocene → ✈

The term 'Anthropocene' refers to a proposed geological epoch. Within this epoch, which encompasses the present day and the near future we are moving towards, the actions of humans – out of all other forms of life – are having the biggest impact on the Earth and its ecosystems. This is due, for the most part, to something called 'anthropogenic climate change', which means global warming caused by human behaviour. Some believe the Anthropocene started with the birth of agriculture over 10,000 years ago, while others think it began with the Industrial Revolution in the 19th century, and still more argue that it began with the first atomic bomb, which was detonated over Hiroshima in 1945 by the US Air Force. The debate continues, nothing is yet set in (geological) stone, and there are many lines of argument around defining the Anthropocene age, or even calling it the 'Anthropocene' at all. Much clearer is the evidence of the harm human beings are inflicting on the planet. The Intergovernmental Panel on Climate Change recently noted that 'the industrial activities that our modern civilization depends upon have raised atmospheric carbon dioxide levels from 280 parts per million to 412 parts per million in the last 150 years'.[1]

F1

The further we remove ourselves from the source of our energy, our food, our clothing and many more day-to-day elements of consumption, the less we understand how much impact our behaviour is having on the planet.

> 'Human beings now largely determine the make-up of the biosphere as well as the chemistry of the atmosphere and oceans, and this episode of the species' dominion will one day be as legible in the fossil record as the advancing ice sheets, asteroid impacts or proliferation of new life-forms that distinguished other epochs.'[2]

Benjamin Kunkel

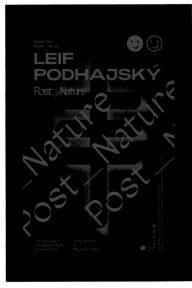

F2

Perhaps to label this age or epoch directly in relation to humanity is, in some way, to legitimize the damage caused: done and dusted, laid down in strata, official. Does it exaggerate the importance of the individual, as opposed to ideology arising from the collective? How much does it take into account socio-political structures and the narratives of consumption driven by capitalist societies that are altering human behaviour on an individual level, spurred on by advances in technology? With increased communication and education, it seems as though we are moving towards a greater awareness of the consequences of consumption while also being exposed to a very effective platform to advertise further consumption. It is a paradox. Ironically, the many confusing and disparate definitions for 'Anthropocene' are describing an age that, at its core, is an age of confusion and vast misinformation, and one that 'struggles with its attention span'[3] in much more than just its geological name.

F1
Dark Star, 2020

F2
Post Nature exhibition flyer, 2019

F3
Aerial photograph of the man-made
Palm Islands in Dubai, UAE

'There's definitely a disconnect between people and the source
of the things we consume, but I think there is also a new movement
to re-establish those connections to our manufacturing and
agricultural systems within the context of modern life. If you take
food, for example, people are becoming more educated on using
local produce, fruit and vegetables that are in season, or those
grown using more sustainable methods of farming. I think this
sort of re-learning is fantastic, as many people are realizing we've
gone too far in the wrong direction and it's bringing about the
destruction of the environmental systems we rely on for survival.
I believe it's a good start, but a lot more can be done and will have
to be done if we are to avoid ecological disaster.'

Leif Podhajsky

Podhajsky's work often pursues a sense of harmony between digital
techniques and organic-feeling outcomes. In 2019, he held a solo
exhibition in London at The Print Space called *Post Nature*, which
explored the ways in which human alteration of the environment is
resulting in new perceptions of what nature is and how we can live within
the new confines of a damaged ecosystem. In these works, the natural
world is presented as being in flux – the imagery investigates resonances
between living and artificial systems, the future cross-pollination of
digital and natural environments, and their impact on us as humans. The
artworks are visions of a symbiotic nature, presenting a hyper-connectivity
between the Earth and machine technology, and posing many questions
about our future on the planet: what will this new digital nature look
and feel like? Will there be a technological singularity that gives way
to AI and the need and desire for a new form of nature? Will we merge
with technology and bring with it the legacy of a past natural world?
The very idea of being post-nature indicates that we might get to a point
where we are beyond our own humanity – because, of course, we are
part of nature.

'I wanted to explore different outcomes of this age, and how
by using technology we might bring about a new symbiosis
with nature.'

Leif Podhajsky

The artworks in this chapter explore a visual manipulation of the world
as we know it. The solid structures we perceive around us are in flux; the
colours are supernatural, vivid and transporting. There is a feeling that
there is a glitch, caught in action, and pieces such as *Post Nature* and
True Vision (pages 192 and 193) evade any particular focal point –
scrambling the vision like a broken screen exposing the fragility of
technological worlds. Other artworks such as *Post Nature :) True Vision*
(page 199) play with symbols that give the illusion of guidance and

F3

signposting certain meanings, but the layered quality of the artwork has an equally disorienting effect. Perhaps it is a pseudo-map to the digital platforms we use to express ourselves – with their runic languages and flowing colours representing a creative freedom underpinned by mathematical grids and code. The combination of flowing forms, almost like liquids swirling in a petri dish, alongside the confines of straight lines and geometric shapes, feels like the application of natural human behaviour to digital systems; natural expression through a lens of technology. Not only are the behaviours and structures humanity has created affecting the balance of the environment, they are also circling back around to affect our natural social behaviours – demonstrating that human beings are part of the natural world that is undergoing such drastic and rapid change.

> 'Education surrounding the environment and an active reconnection to nature is important, as it makes us realize we are part of nature, not separate from it, and this is a major factor to overcome with things like climate change. Once we as humans can re-establish this connection I think we can start to bring about a change in how we use the planet and its resources.'

Leif Podhajsky

Podhajsky has a huge collection of *National Geographic* magazines, inherited from his grandfather, which he often draws on for inspiration. The volumes create a kind of Yellow Brick Wall in his Berlin apartment, leading to stories and photographs from every corner of the globe. The magazine was created to cover topics ranging from science and geography to history and world culture, and aims to both 'illuminate and protect'[4] the wonders of the world around us, outside any immediate or individual location. Since the National Geographic Society was founded in 1888, 132 years ago, the global human population has grown from 1.5 billion to the staggering number of over 7.6 billion people. 'As a result, we are in the process of dismantling the major ecosystems that are essential to maintaining not only the world's human culture, but also all life on Earth.'[5] As we enter the sixth phase of extinction, it seems that one way forward is to give a platform to threatened species and environments, to educate older generations and younger generations alike. Art is a way to elevate these issues and place them in front of an audience.

> 'Especially since becoming a father, that feeling of anxiety about the health of the world we are passing on has definitely affected my work. I feel, even more so, the importance of developing and showcasing nature within my work.'

Leif Podhajsky

F4
A photograph of the Rheinische Braunkohlerevier mine in Germany. The dismantling of the brown coal with a surface mining method altered the landscape and led to the formation of several major industrial sites

F5
A photograph showing coral bleaching

F6
An illustration created by NASA as part of their theoretical 'Space Colonies' project in the 1970s

F4

F5

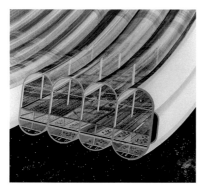

F6

1. NASA, 'The Causes of Climate Change', https://climate.nasa.gov/causes/ [accessed 26 July 2020]
2. Benjamin Kunkel, 'The Capitalocene', *London Review of Books*, vol. 39, no. 5, 2 March 2017, https://www.lrb.co.uk/the-paper/v39/n05/benjamin-kunkel/the-capitalocene?referrer=https%3A%2F%2Fwww.google.com%2F [accessed 26 July 2020]
3. Kunkel, Ibid.
4. *National Geographic*, 'About Us', https://www.nationalgeographic.org/about-us/ [accessed 26 July 2020]
5. *National Geographic*, Ibid.

'Education surrounding the environment and an active reconnection to nature is important, as it makes us realize we are part of nature … '

↪ Leif Podhajsky

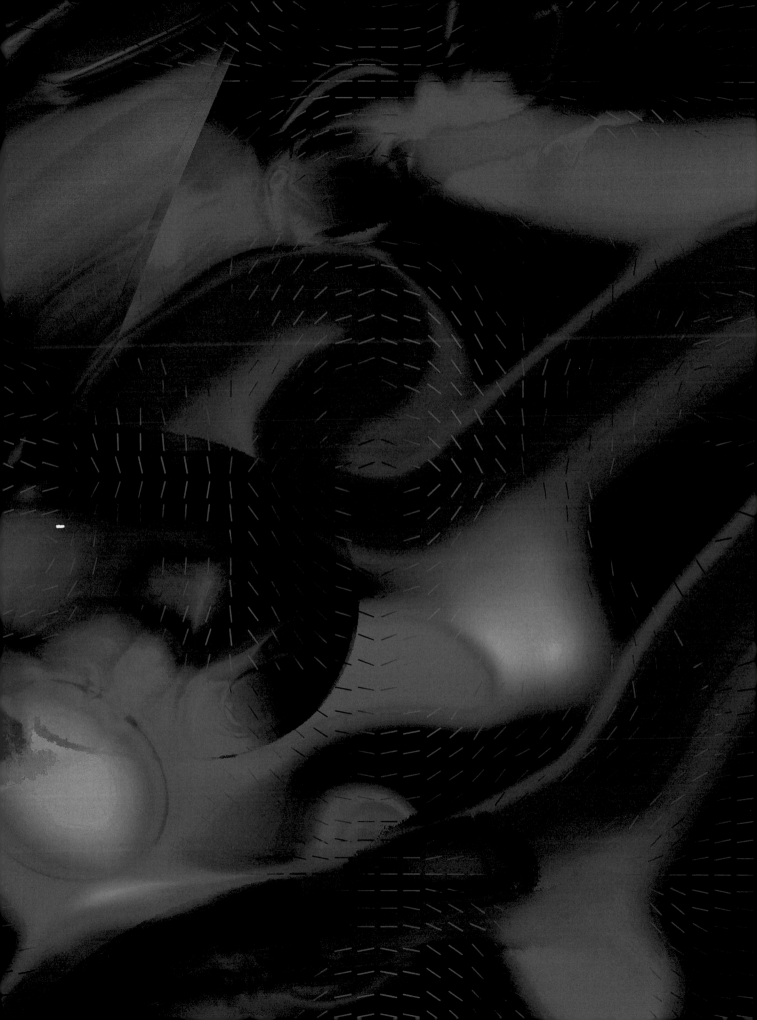

02

05

Digital Aura, 2019

05
Digital Aura II, 2019

'Especially since becoming a father, that feeling of anxiety about the health of the world we are passing on has definitely affected my work'

↪ Leif Podhajsky

Impaired Visions, 2020

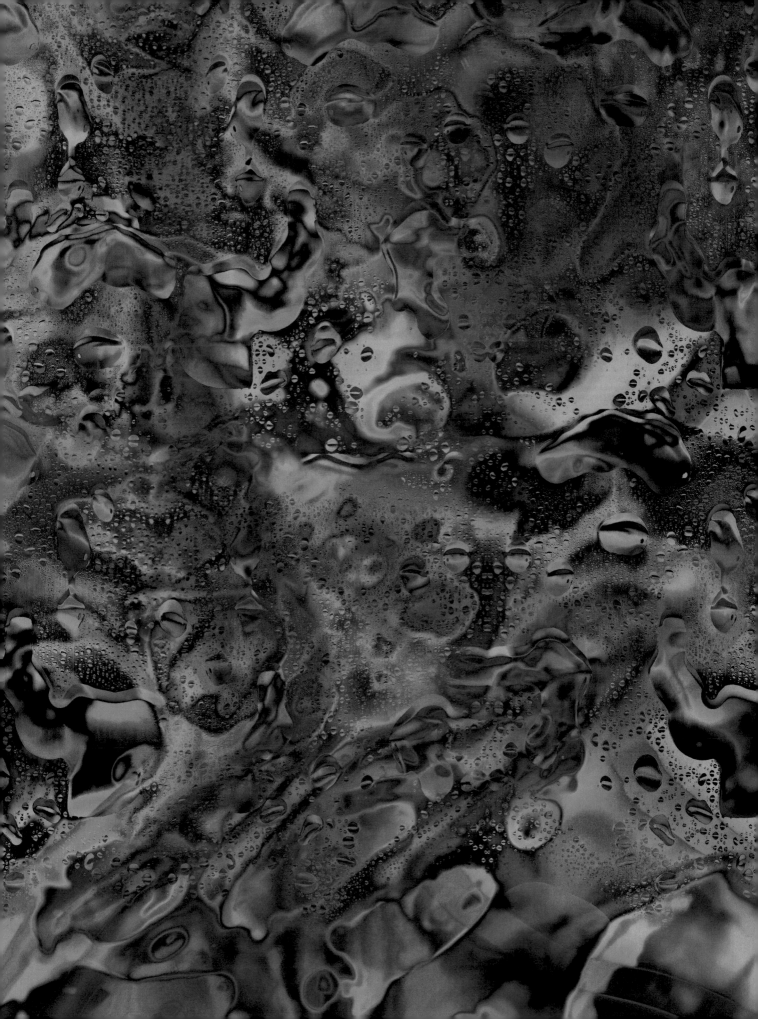

08

08
ACiD brb, 2020

09 →
Post Nature :) True Vision, 2020

ExtremeVisions
Sudden Action
True Vision
True Nature
Impaired Visions
Visual Impairment
Visual Bloom
B-Sides
Sudden Extreme
System Output
System Outputs
Genetic Predisposition

→   →   →

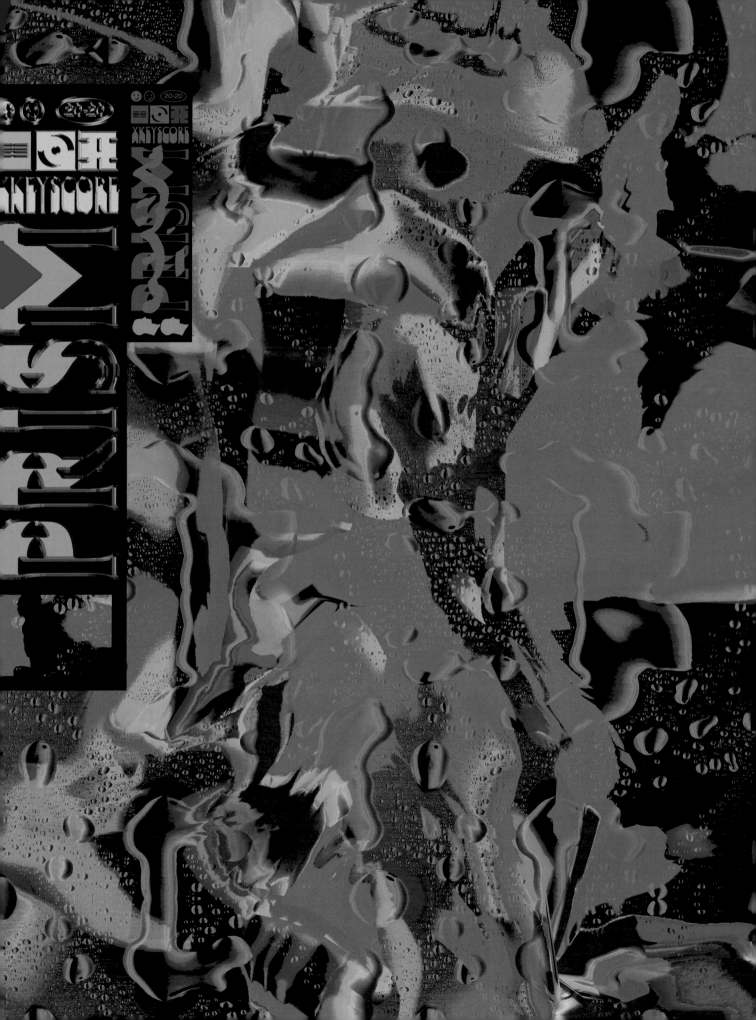

11

← 10

PRISM, 2020

11

PHOS_STAR, 2020

12

12

Alien Interface Grafik, 2020

13 ⟶

Lil Uzi ReMake, 2020

'People are realizing we've gone too far in the wrong direction and it's bringing about the destruction of the environmental systems we rely on for survival'

↪ Leif Podhajsky

Dark Skies, 2020

15

15

Deepspace, 2020

16 →

Post Nature :) True Vision II, 2020

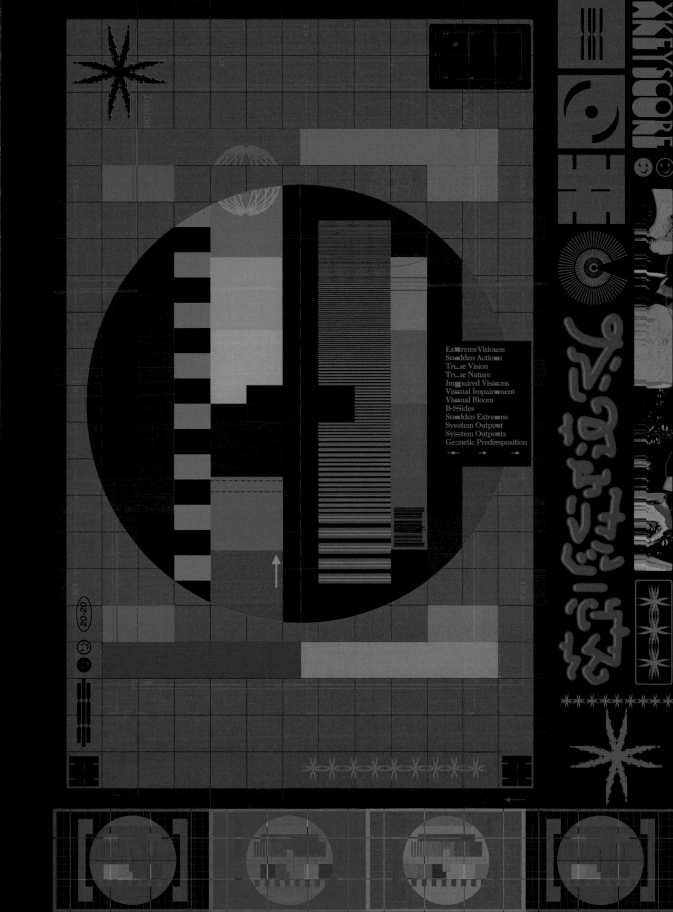

ExtremeVisions
Sudden Action
True Vision
True Nature
Impaired Visions
Visual Impairment
Visual Bloom
B-Sides
Sudden Extreme
System Output
System Outputs
Genetic Predisposition

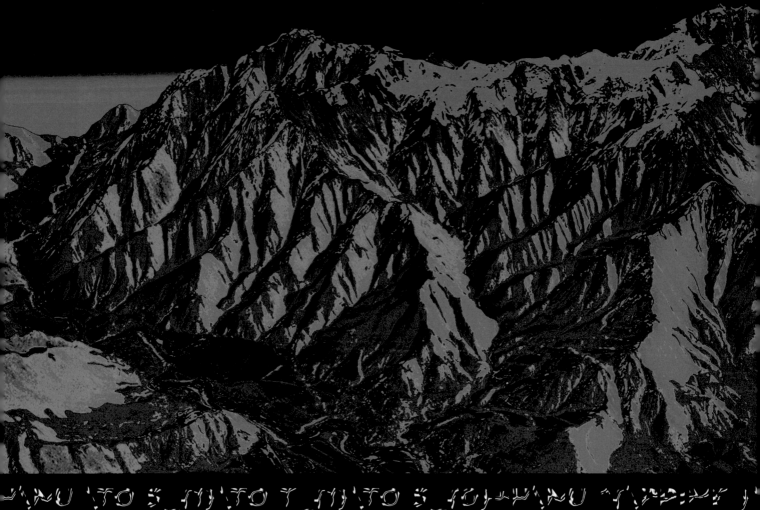

EDITION NUMBER	EDITION SIZE	PRINT NAME	STOCK
**			

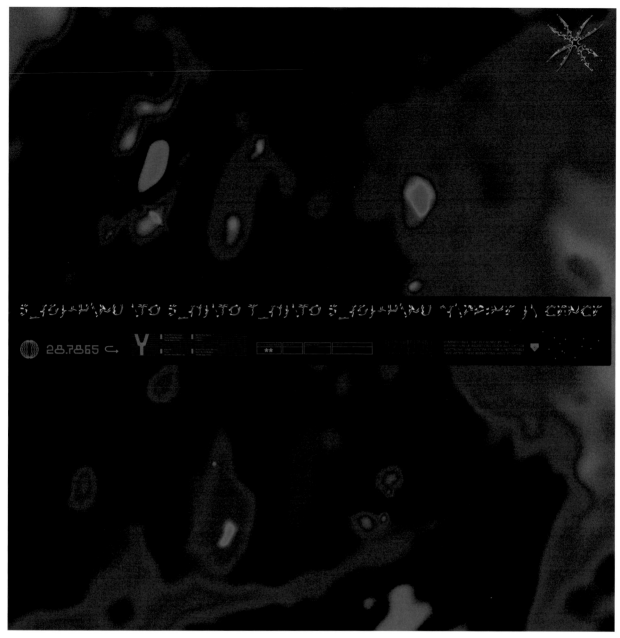

18

← 17

Light Absorption, 2020

18

Heat Map, 2020

19 ↓

Alien Interface , 2020

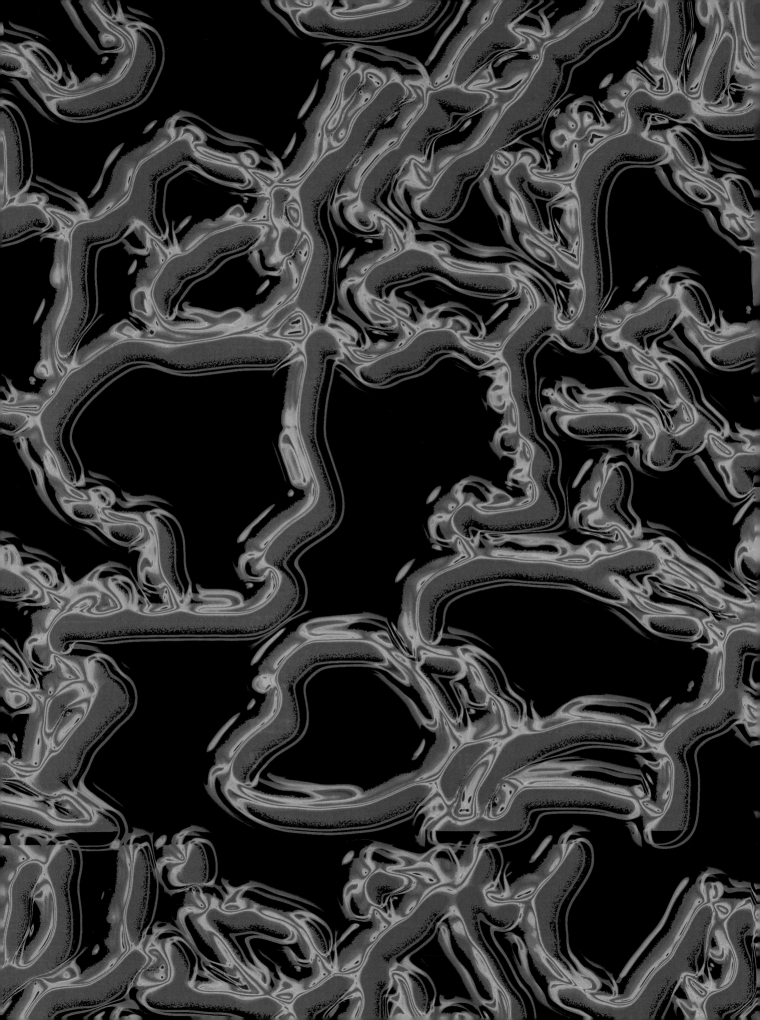

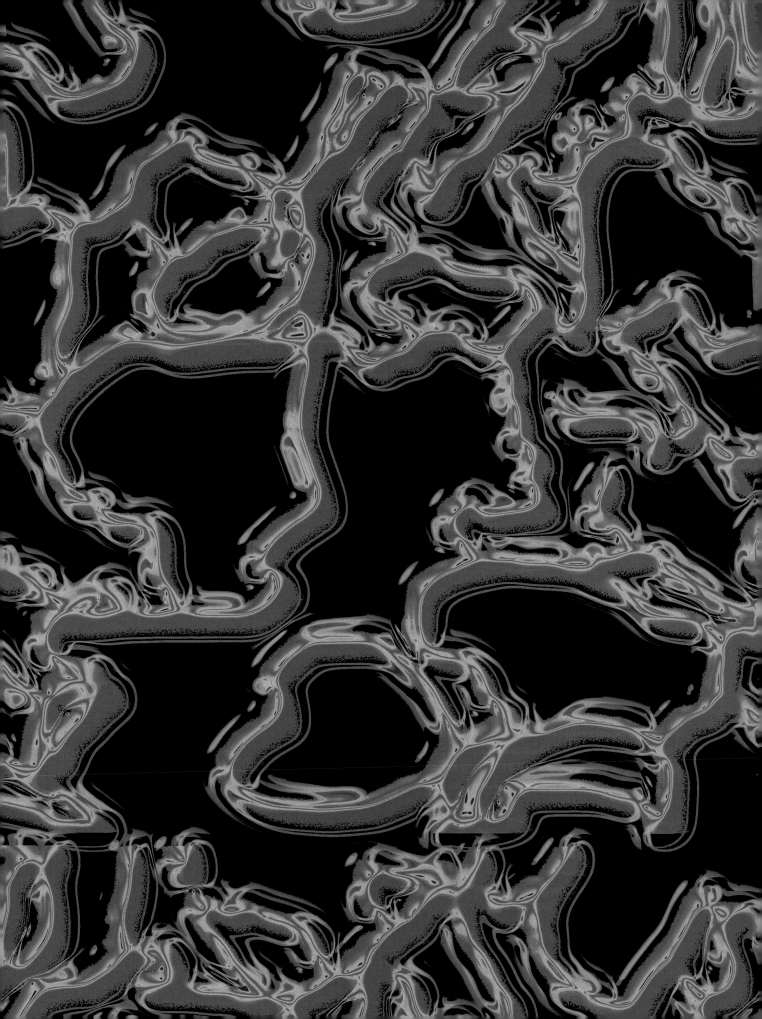

YOU WITH AIR
YOUNG MAGIC
2010
Carpark Records
CAK 58

EXPECTATION
TAME IMPALA
2010
Modular Recordings

SOLITUDE IS BLISS
TAME IMPALA
2010
Modular Recordings
MODVL127

GILGAMESH
GYPSY & THE CAT
2010
Sony
CAT 88697

INNERSPEAKER
TAME IMPALA
2010
Modular Recordings
MODVL128 / MODCD126

WOUNDED RHYMES
LYKKE LI
2011
Atlantic
5052498451173

LUCIDITY
TAME IMPALA
2010
Modular Recordings
MODVL128

NIGHT IN THE OCEAN
YOUNG MAGIC
2011
Carpark Records
CAK 69

WHY WON'T YOU MAKE
UP YOUR MIND
TAME IMPALA
2010
Modular Recordings
MODVL139

WIM
WIM
2011
Modular Recordings
MODCD140

FUTURE PRIMITIVE
THE VINES
2011
Sony
88697925212

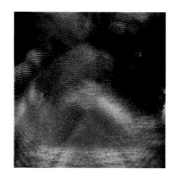

TOY
TOY
2012
Heavenly
HVNLP94/HVNLP94CD

FROM NOWHERE
DAN CROLL
2011
Racquet Records
RAC001

LIVE AT KEXP
SHABAZZ PALACES
2012
Sub-Pop
SP995

REMIXES
PEAKING LIGHTS
2011
Domino/Weird World
WEIRD010T

DRY LAND IS NOT A MYTH
WHITE ARROWS
2012
Caroline Records
VTV-002/530525-2

IN GHOSTLIKE FADING
MY BEST FRIEND
2012
Warp Records
WARP LP224/WARP CD224

NEED IT
SPLASHH
2012
Luv Luv Luv
3711041

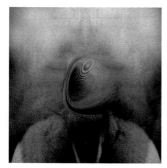

MELT
YOUNG MAGIC
2012
Carpark Records
CAK 72

OWLLE
DISORDER
2012
Sony

LONERISM
TAME IMPALA
2012
Modular Recordings
MODVL161

HOLY FIRE
FOALS
2013
Transgressive Records
LC 14666

APOCOLYPSE DREAMS
TAME IMPALA
2012
Modular Recordings
MRTIAD001

THE NORTH BORDERS
BONOBO
2013
Ninja Tune
ZEN195/ZENCD195

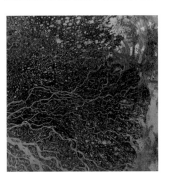

FEELS LIKE WE ONLY GO
BACKWARDS
TAME IMPALA
2012
Modular Recordings
MODVL173

CIRRUS
BONOBO
2013
Ninja Tune
ZEN12357

ELEPHANT
TAME IMPALA
2012
Modular Recordings
MODVL166

FIRST FIRES
BONOBO
2013
Ninja Tune
ZEN12366

MIND MISCHIEF
TAME IMPALA
2013
Modular Recordings
MODVL175AMPO

TEN TIGERS
BONOBO
2013
Ninja Tune
ZEN12379

BIRDS OF TOKYO
MARCH FIRES
2013
EMI Records
7253982/7253981

FRANCE
OWLLE
2014
Sony
88843028551/
88725461892

COLD SPRING FAULT
LESS YOUTH
MOUNT KIMBIE
2013
Warp Records
WARPLP237/WARP CD237

FOOD
KELIS
2014
Ninja Tune
ZEN205/7FN205CD

DREAM CAVE
CLOUD CONTROL
2013
Infectious Music
INFECT163LP/
INFECT163CDP

BREATHING STATUES
YOUNG MAGIC
2014
Carpark Records
CAK95/CAK95p

WHEN THE NIGHT
ST LUCIA
2013
Neon Gold
88883769261/
88883769262

CLOSER
EVY JANE
2014
Ninja Tune
ZEN12384

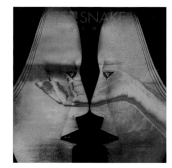

GLOW
TENSNAKE
2014
Virgin EMI Records
V3123/CDV3123

CLOUD BOAT
MODEL OF YOU
2014
Apollo Records
AMB1409LP/AMB1409CD

KARA
WE ARE SHINING
2014
Marathon Artists
MA0027LP/MA0027CDRT

CRYSTALS
OF MONSTERS AND MEN
2015
Republic Records

FLASHLIGHT
BONOBO
2014
Ninja Tune
ZEN12409

BLEEDS
ROOTS MANUVA
2015
Ninja Tune/Big Dada
BD269/BDCD269P

ALL WE ARE
ALL WE ARE
2015
Double Six
DS091LP

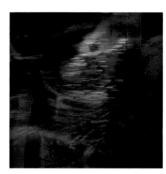

SOUNDTRACK
FASTER THAN LIGHT
2015
iAm8Bit
8BIT-8008

ELSEWHERE
DENAI MOORE
2015
Because Music
BEC5156011 / BEC5156007

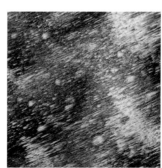

SOUNDTRACK
(ADVANCED EDITION)
FASTER THAN LIGHT
2015
iAm8Bit
8BIT-8018

BENEATH THE SKIN
OF MONSTERS AND MEN
2015
Republic Records
472742-5/472850-1

HENRI TEXIER - LES LÀ-BAS
(BONOBO REMIX)
BONOBO
2016
Ninja Tune
ZEN12432

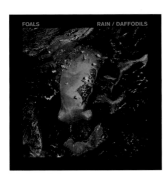

RAIN / DAFFODILS
FOALS
2016
Warner Records/
Transgressive Records
0825646484959/
0825646484959

GOLDEN
KYLIE MINOGUE
2018
BMG
538360711/538360801

IT IS
JMSN
2016
White Room Records
WRR012/WRR011

SUCK ON LIGHT
BOY & BEAR
2019
Island Records/
Universal Music
7793504/7793504

TKAY
TKAY
2016
Dew Process/
Kitsuné Music
DEW9000996/CDB-068

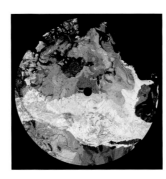

LANGATA
CROOKED COLOURS
2019
Sweat It Out
SWEATA019V/SWEATA014

TRUTH IS A BEAUTIFUL
THING
LONDON GRAMMAR
2017
Ministry Of Sound
MADART2LTD/MADART2

DUALITY
DUKE DUMONT
2020
Virgin/EMI
V3243/CDV3243

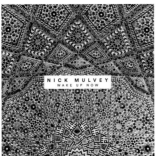

WAKE UP NOW
NICK MULVEY
2017
Caroline Records
MULVEY013/MULVEY014

ACKNOWLEDGEMENTS

I'd like to thank Evie Tarr: without your vision and support, this book would never have come to life. Thank you for believing in the work and making the process such an adventure.

Also thanks to Darren Wall and Lucas Dietrich, and the entire team(s) at Volume and Thames & Hudson for all the hard work and trust. And to Peter Dawson and Amy Shortis at Grade for the stellar design work.

To all the bands, musicians and record labels that I've worked with over the years, thank you for the trust and combined creative experiences. It's been a true pleasure to create artwork for such wonderful and historic music releases.

A deep thank you to everyone who has followed my work and journey over the years. I'm constantly floored by how it has connected with so many of you. To all those who contributed to the book, it feels right that this is a product of your support and encouragement.

To my family and friends for everything.

To my love, Sophie: I really couldn't have done it without your love over the years. For lifting me up when I lose confidence in the vision, and putting up with my grumpiness. To Freya (sister), Avan (brother), Antony (Dad) and Jane (Mum).

Mum, a special thanks for encouraging and nurturing my creative side throughout my life; I wouldn't be here without you.

And to my beautiful daughter, Scout! This is for you. I hope I make you proud.

x

All pictures by Leif Podhajsky apart from the following

Introduction
F1 U.S. Fish and Wildlife Service, Gary M. Stolz
F2 Erik Fenderson
F3 Material from the S.F. ORACLE provided courtesy of the Estate of Allen Cohen and Regent Press, publishers of the SAN FRANCISCO ORACLE FACSIMILE EDITION (Digital Version) available at www.regentpress.net./CC-BY-SA-3.0
F4 Manuscripts and Archives Division, The New York Public Library. *Plotting circle* (1962–1964) retrieved from http://digitalcollections.nypl.org/items/c7f5a790-5389-0135-3b45-3fd34c6ef837

Tame Impala
10, 11, 13, 14, 16 Original photographs by Kevin Parker
12, 14 Original photograph by Matthew C. Saville

Synesthesia
F1 Optics: spectra of various substances. Coloured process print by R. H. Digeon, *c.* 1868., Wellcome Collection, Attribution 4.0 International (CC BY 4.0)
F3 Diagram, based on Gino Casagrande (2004) and modified by Dr Hugo Heyrman (2005), doctorhugo.org
F4 Emily Noyes Vanderpoel, Smithsonian Libraries
F5 Peter M. Maloca, Christian Schwaller, Ruslan Hlushchuk, Sébastien Barré, OCTlab University of Basel/Bern and Royal Moorfields Eye Hospital, London. Attribution 4.0 International (CC BY 4.0)
F6 *Optics: spectra of various substances.* Illustration by R. H. Digeon, *c.* 1868., Wellcome Collection, Attribution 4.0 International (CC BY 4.0)
F7 Annie Besant, Charles Leadbeater, Project Gutenberg

Foals
04 Original photograph by Steve Gullick
01, 07, 08 Original photograph by Thomas Nebbia

Nature
F1 Antony Podhajsky
F6 Bob Blaylock/CC-BY-SA-3.0
F7 Nehemiah Grew, Missouri Botanical Garden

Lykke Li
01–05 Original photographs by Roger Deckker

London Grammar
Page 165 and 01–07 Original photographs by Elliot Lee Hazel

Digital Ritual
F1 Matt Britt/CC-BY-SA-3.0
F2 National Cancer Institute/CC-BY-SA-3.0
F3 Joseph Lertola/CC-BY-SA-3.0
F4 Gindelis/CC-BY-SA-3.0
F5 MartinThoma/CC0
F6 'Gathering' by Jacek Zmarz, 2018

Anthropocene
F3 Skatebiker/CC-BY-SA-4.0
F4 Tobias Mandt
F5 The Ocean Agency/XL Catlin Seaview Survey/Richard Vevers/CC-BY-2.0
F6 NASA, https://settlement.arc.nasa.gov/70sArt/art.html

BIBLIOGRAPHY

Cox, Lisa, 'Great Barrier Reef suffers 89% collapse in new coral after bleaching events', *Guardian*, 3 April 2019, https://www.theguardian.com/environment/2019/apr/04/great-barrier-reef-suffers-89-collapse-in-new-coral-after-bleaching-events [accessed 21 July 2020]

Ehrlich, Gretel, *The Solace of Open Spaces*, Penguin (1986)

Huxley, Aldous, *The Doors of Perception*, Vintage (2004, first published 1954)

Jarman, Derek, *Chroma: A Book of Colour*, The Overlook Press (1995)

Jay, Mike, *Mescaline: A Global History of the First Psychedelic*, Yale University Press (2019)

Kandinsky, Wassily, translated by Michael T. H. Sadler, *Concerning the Spiritual in Art*, Project Gutenberg (2011), http://www.gutenberg.org/cache/epub/5321/pg5321-images.html [accessed 20 July 2020]

Kunkel, Benjamin, 'The Capitalocene', *London Review of Books*, vol. 39, no. 5, 2 March 2017, https://www.lrb.co.uk/the-paper/v39/n05/benjamin-kunkel/the-capitalocene?referrer=https%3A%2F%2Fwww.google.com%2F [accessed 26 July 2020]

Lanier, Jaron, 'What Makes the Public Square Square?', *The Future of Public Space: SOM Thinkers Series*, Metropolis Books (2018)

MacFarland, Matt, 'Google's psychedelic "paint brush" raises the oldest question in art', *The Washington Post*, 10 March 2016, https://www.washingtonpost.com/news/innovations/wp/2016/03/10/googles-psychedelic-paint-brush-raises-the-oldest-question-in-art/ [accessed 21 July 2020]

Martin, Andy, 'In search of the Sixties: Was the decade really as good as we think it was?', *Independent*, 15 September 2017, https://www.independent.co.uk/news/long_reads/sixties-decade-was-it-good-sexual-revolution-swinging-london-hippies-culture-music-art-germaine-a7946506.html [accessed 20 July 2020]

NASA, 'The Causes of Climate Change', https://climate.nasa.gov/causes/ [accessed 26 July 2020]

National Geographic, 'About Us', https://www.nationalgeographic.org/about-us/ [accessed 26 July 2020]

Pollan, Michael, *How to Change Your Mind: The New Science of Psychedelics*, Penguin (2018)

Ross, Hannah, Farrow-Smith, Elloise and Herbert, Bronwyn, 'Byron Bay's Bundjalung people celebrate long-awaited land and sea native title determination', ABC News, 30 April 2019, https://www.abc.net.au/news/2019-04-30/byron-bay-native-title-land-rights/11057896 [accessed 21 July 2020]

Stamets, Paul, 'Mushrooms, Mycology of Consciousness', EcoFarm Conference Keynote, 2017, https://www.youtube.com/watch?v=t8DjeaU8eMs [accessed 21 July 2020]

Tett, Gillian, 'How ancient rituals help us adapt to the digital age', *Financial Times*, https://www.ft.com/content/c3a55ae0-9797-11e9-9573-ee5cbb98ed36 [accessed 21 July 2020]

Witt, Emily, 'The Unpredictable Cactus', *London Review of Books*, vol. 42, no. 1, 2 January 2020, https://www.lrb.co.uk/the-paper/v42/n01/emily-witt/the-unpredictable-cactus [accessed 20 July 2020]

Rozina Aamir
Kieran Ahmed
James Albanesr
Shah Ali
Gabe Alvare
Jonny Ames
Chuck Anderson
Sergio Arceo
Freddie Armitage
Iom Armstrong
Natalia Avdeeva
Michael Avent
Joshua Babcock
Rémy Badout
Lily Bailie
Peter Charles Edward
   Baker
Scotty Baker
Almudena Ballarin
Joseph Ballouz
Jeremy Baranowski-Grey
Lewis Barnes
Grant Barron
Tyler Barron
Jake Barry
Samantha Basar
Claire-Lise Beiner
Jack Bendall
David Benge
Tom Bentley
Tobias Bergholm
Emelie Birgersson
Alex Birks
Evan Bishop
Fabricio Bizu Psych BR
Darryn Blackford
Cameron Blackmore
Pru Bleasdale
Liam Blenkinsop
Kaleb Boback-Clark
Cole Bodell
Avery Booker
Brian Booker
Fraser Borowski
Erik Brady
Ciara Lea Claudio
   Braganza
Braguette Collectif
Jordan Braithwaite
Zane Brewer
Lauren Brobin & Courtney
   Farrell

AG Brooks
Rickey Brooksher
Norman Brosterman
Ashley Brown
Benjamin Brown
Jade Brown
Peter Brünings-Hansen
Alexander Buchta
Finn Buick
Stefan Bullones
Brooks Burgoon
Ryan Burns
Samm Butler
Garrett C
Peter Cahlstadt
Shona Cairns
Perry Callaghan
Jose Camacho
Lynden Campbell
Nicolas Campbell
Matías Candia
Paloma Canut
Riccardo Carlet
Robert Carmichael
Paul Carter
Regina Cervantes
Louise Chambers
Giles Chandler
Lola Charpentier
Simon Chaussard
Dan Chillari
Mary Christopherson
Adam Cicchini
Amanda Clark
Callum Clarke
Rob Clough
Diana Colangelo
Alex Cole
Hannah Colson
Liam Connor
Aidan Conway
Emily Copp
Cedric Coudyser
Dermot Cox
James Cox
Connor Crawford
Adam Crins
Frances Cruz
Francisca Cruz
Tom Cullum
Sam Cutler
Kamil Czapiga

Jonathan Daly
Dominicus Damaran
Dank
Brian Danos
Steven Dao Lan Mach
Noémie Darveau
Paul Davin
Jordan Christopher Day
Matthew De Jong
Richard de Ruijter
Máximo de Vries
Alex Deamon
Bertrand Decrion
Henrik Degerman Jonsson
Madelon Doest
Mark Doherty
Grace Ducas
Annabelle Dunbar-
   Whittaker
Charley Dupont
Natasha Durley
Jerome Dwyer
John Dwyer
Jessica Edmiston
Mark Edwards
Miles Elliott
Ryan Ellis
Alex Engelgau
Roger Estrada
Luc Fafard
Daniel Fairley
Alex Fassone
Emile Fedeczko
Omri Feinstein
Guillermo Fernandez
Mitch Fielder
Alexander Finch
Chris Finnerty
Charlie Fisher
Hannah FitzSimons
Thomas Fleck
David Fleming
Gabriella Fountain
Tom Fournier
Ben Fraser
TJ Freda
Gabriel Buchmann Freire
Caspar David Friedrich
Jordan Friel
Mitchell Fuller & Rachael
   Lopez
Function Store

Jarod Funk
Daniel Fyffe
Thomas Gabriel
Vincent Galinier
Nik Gandhi
Dom Garcia
Carolina Garcia Paladino
Ash Gardner
Luke Garnet
Brett Garrett
Sam Garry
Katharine Gaspar
Ethan Gatehouse
August Gaukstad
Chris Geddes
Valentin Gény
Ian Geraghty
Rory Gillespie
Briana Gillies
Sam Gilling
Cameron Gleave
Mark Glogowski
Ryan Godfrey
Moses Goh
Martin Gonzalez
Huntly Gordon
Sabina Goth
Jonas Grahl
Matthew Brian Gray
Amanda Greene
Jon Griffiths
David Grima
Chrissy Groeneweg
Stanisław Gruszczyński
John Hairston
Cody Hale
Isaak Haley
Jaimeson Hall
Thomas Hall
NM Hanan
Jason Hancock
Tyrone Hansen
Jake Hansle
Riana J Harley
Jed Harling
Evan Harris
Kristofer Harris
Monica Harrison
Tom Harrison
Conor Hars
Nelson Hassinger
Jeremiah Hayes

Perry Prineas
Oli Proctor
Kirian Procyk
Adam Pryor
Brooke Qualman
John Radnell
Tiffani Rael
Raised By Snakes
James Rajaratnam
Axel Ramirez
James Ramlal
Jair Ramos
Raul D Ramos
Jeremy Raskin
Thomas Rasp
Jay Ratcliffe
Brandon Rattan
Rebecca
Gaëtan Recly
Red + t
Carl Regan
Justin Reicherdt
Tiago Reis
Alexandra Reisig
Christian Reyes
Derek Reyes
Benjamin Reynolds
Pavel Rezakov
Ben Rice
Travis Rice
Paolo Rinaldi
Maxime Ritter
James Roberts
Adam Robertson
Tom Robey
Francisco Rodriguez
Axel Roessler
James Rogerson
Blaž Rojs
Alex Roka
Chris Romano
Daniel Roque
Evariste Roussel
Adam Royce
Lauren Rushton
Jack Ryan
Stephen Syren Ryan
Chad Sabo
Anna Sachs
Nick Samaan
Tomas Samsøe
Henry Saunderson

Såvvy
Jannis Schäfer
Fabrizia Schettino
Fabian Schläfli
Kim Schläpfer
Morgan Schlosser
Avery Schneidt
Ed Schofield
Pedro Schuller
Kane Scott
Leo Scott
Zack Scott
Gabriel Seabra
Nick Seeds
Thomas Selwood
Jana Sempels
Ryan Shacklette
Jacob Shafer
Amy Shaffer
Joseph Sharples
Keeley Sheppard
Daniel Shinaman
Neel Shivdasani
Stefan Sieder
Colin Siert
Maria Luigia Silvano
Simon
Beau Sims
Megan Sinkinson
    Withrow
Jonas Skafte
Jasper Smit
Cameron Johnathon
    David Smith
Dylan Smith
Ryan Smith
Joshua Söhn
Daniel Somlo
Liliya Sotirova
Charlotte Elizabeth
    Sowerby
Jordan Sowers
Ben Spenceley
Claudia Speranza
Nicola Spokes
Cooper Springfield
Steve Stacey
Deborah Stack
Giorgio Stagi
Blake Stassi
Kyle Stead
Christina Steely

Nikita Stepanyuk
Thomas Stoker
Jake Stoughton
Jacob Straffon
Morten Strømme
Simon Stroud
Joe Sullivan
Lasse Surland
Josh Swancutt
Alex Swartwout
Nancy Szachno-
    Dressel
Cesar Taillardat
Raul Tellegen
theFranks
James Thomas
Scott Thompson
Will Timney
Olly Townsend
Owen Tozer
Pascal Tran Binh
John Treinen
Aurelien Trevisan
Ayumi Tsushida
Sanjay Twisk
Rocco Tyndale
Adam Ugarkovic
Lorenzo Uribe
James Usill
Patrick Valiquette
Antoine Van Aken
James Van Camp
James van den
    Elshout
Willem van der
    Schoot
Nicholas
    Vandenberg
Michael Vassari
Amaury Vedis
Juan Pedro
    Villanueva
    Holm-Nielsen
Myriam Villar
Tihomir Vrbanec
Jack Walker
Claudia Walraven
Josh Wangrud
Marcus Watkinson
James Webb
Eric Wefer
Linn Weile

Daniel Whillas
Andy White
Ash White
Miah Whiteaker
Baudouin Willemart
David Williams
Jamie Williams
Juli Williams
Matthew Williamson
Tom Willis
Anfisa Wilson
Stuart Wilson
Theo Witrylak
Joel Woodford
Devin Wright
Xander & Marine
Taylor Yacobucci
YummyColours
Nicole Zabik
Kyle Zamberlin
Patryk Zasadzki
Marion Zitoli
Antonia Zuruev
吳宜樺

About the Artist

Leif Podhajsky is an Australian graphic designer, artist and art director, known for the distinctive album covers he has designed for some of the past decade's biggest electronic, indie and psychedelic artists. His striking style has also attracted leading brands, such as Nike and Ralph Lauren, and the likes of Sydney Opera House, where he has exhibited his ethereal video installations and designs as part of the Vivid LIVE festival since 2016. Podhajsky grew up surrounded by the waterfalls and rainforests of Byron Bay, and has since lived in Melbourne, London and, presently, Berlin.

About the Writer

Evie Tarr is a writer, editor and musician based in London.

On the cover: *Digital Aura*, 2019

This edition first published in the United Kingdom in 2021 by Thames & Hudson Ltd, 181A High Holborn, London WC1V 7QX

First published in the United States of America in 2021 by Thames & Hudson Inc., 500 Fifth Avenue, New York, New York 10110

New Psychedelia © 2021 Thames & Hudson Ltd, London
Artwork by Leif Podhajsky © 2021 Leif Podhajsky
For all other illustrations, please see the picture credits on page 219

Design and layout by Peter Dawson, Amy Shortis, gradedesign.com
Art direction and cover design by Leif Podhajsky
Written by Evie Tarr

British Library Cataloguing-in-Publication Data
A catalogue record for this book is available from the British Library

Library of Congress Control Number 2020940903

ISBN   978-0-500-02402-7

Printed and bound in China by Artron Art (Group) Co., Ltd

Be the first to know about our new releases, exclusive content and author events by visiting
thamesandhudson.com
thamesandhudsonusa.com
thamesandhudson.com.au